W9-CPB-742

THE ASTROLOGY SOURCEBOOK

THE
ASTROLOGY
SOURCEBOOK

A Guide to the Symbolic Language of the Stars

SHIRLEY SOFFER

LOWELL HOUSE

LOS ANGELES

NTC/Contemporary Publishing Group

Library of Congress Cataloging-in-Publication Data

Soffer, Shirley
    The astrology sourcebook / by Shirley Soffer.
        p.   cm.
    Includes bibliographical references (p.   ) and index.
    ISBN 1-56565-883-3
        1. Astrology.   I. Title.
    BF1708. 1 .S64 1998
    133.5—dc21   98-45095
                                                                      CIP

Published by Lowell House, a division of NTC/Contemporary Publishing Group, Inc.
4255 West Touhy Avenue, Lincolnwood, Illinois 60646-1975 U.S.A.

Copyright © 1998 by Shirley Soffer and NTC/Contemporary Publishing Group.
All rights reserved. No part of this work may be reproduced, stored in a retrieval system,
or transmitted in any form or by any means electronic, mechanical, photocopying,
recording, or otherwise without prior permission of NTC/Contemporary Publishing
Group, Inc.

Requests for such permissions should be addressed to:
Lowell House
2020 Avenue of the Stars, Suite 300
Los Angeles, CA 90067

Design by Laurie Young
Illustrations by Paul Janovsky

Printed and bound in the United States of America
International Standard Book Number: 1-56565-883-3

10 9 8 7 6 5 4 3 2 1

HOMER TWP. PUBLIC LIBRARY DIST.
14320 W. 151st STREET
LOCKPORT, ILLINOIS 60441

To *the stars in my firmament:*

Simeon, Karen, and Haley

✧ ✧

Sarah, Peter, and Samuel

"The least of things with a meaning is always worth more
in life than the greatest of things without it."

—CARL G. JUNG

acknowledgments

THE PERSON MOST RESPONSIBLE FOR LAUNCHING THIS BOOK IS MY FRIEND AND teacher, Eileen McCabe. It was Eileen who strongly insisted I take on the project, assuring me I could do it. Eileen has consistently encouraged my efforts in astrology, and I thank her for everything.

In earlier years, prior to my becoming an astrologer, my friend Daphne Mumford Duback believed in me sufficiently to assist me financially as a writer. By way of this book, I have finally fulfilled my pledge to Daphne, and I thank her for standing by me back then, when I needed it most.

Although writing is a solitary enterprise, the process was greatly eased for me by a supportive astrological community. My clients and students were always with me in spirit as I worked, rooting me on. And so many of my colleagues offered words of encouragement and showed interest in my progress. I wish I could list them all.

My family, to whom this book is dedicated, was a constant resource. Peter Liberman, in particular, lent his formidable editing skills and sharp intellect to the task, always spurring me on to do better. I owe him my deepest thanks.

Sarah Jane Horton, Judi Vitale, Larry Howard, and Carolyn Goldhush were my computer gurus, each in their separate ways contributing much-needed technical expertise. I thank them for their patience and calming good humor.

I also want to thank Jenny Seymore for her kind words of referral to Bud Sperry of Lowell House, who proposed the book project to me on her good recommendation. At Lowell House, Maria Magallanes guided me gently and sensitively through the editorial process, for which she has my gratitude.

Finally, I want to acknowledge Mary Evans's generosity. Her publishing experience and knowledge, openly given, helped me enormously at the onset of the project. I am extremely grateful to her.

contents

introduction

LIVING THE SYMBOLIC LIFE

Every one of us has a story to tell—a life story. But we cannot always find the words to tell it. Astrology gives us a language for our story because it shows us that our life has a plot, a kind of invisible design that becomes more apparent if we pay close attention to its patterning.

Central to this plot is character, *our* character. For as any storyteller knows, it is not just how the plot unfolds but how the person in the story interacts with it. What is the person thinking, feeling, or believing? Will he or she grow, learn, or change in the course of events? If so, how? If not, why not? How much does character impinge on plot? Or plot on character? Are they each implacably fixed, fated? And in the final telling, is character itself a form of fate?

There is no single—or simple—answer to these questions. Astrology, in telling our story, does not provide a neat denouement, a final wrap-up of the conflicts and complexities our story may reveal because like life itself, our story does not resolve itself easily. It is still being told as its plot unfolds.

In other words, our story as told in the language of astrology is really a process. Its product is self-discovery; its character is always *you*. The language of astrology is written in the first-person singular. Who am I in my intrinsic nature? How do I typically respond to life's challenges? Where do I put most of my energies? When can I expect results from my efforts? What are my coping devices, my behavior patterns?

WHAT IS ASTROLOGY?

Why? That is the question that remains unanswered. Only you, in piecing together the various chapters of your story, have the ultimate ability to extract meaning from it. Using your own internal measurement, only you can determine the happy ending, the tragic downfall, or the comedic pratfall in your ongoing story. That is how your character develops as it grapples with its plot. Astrology simply weaves character and plot together to tell your story.

Astrology is not a moral tale, a religious tract, a karmic catalog, or a guide to self-mastery. It is not a method of control—of self, others, or the events that inevitably fall in front of your doorstep. Astrology simply traces your life's key episodes, and how you, as the central character, tend to deal with them.

In doing so it helps you become aware of yourself because in the telling of your story, astrology creates a mirror for you to reflect upon. And in seeing yourself you are somehow also seen and validated—perhaps by some other part of yourself that you may have lost sight of. In the process, the fullness of your character emerges; you are put back whole, re-membered. Something is awakened in your psyche and brought to life simply by the act of looking at yourself in that mirror, which astrology calls the "horoscope." The horoscope, then, is a kind of cosmic mirror that visually connects you to your life story as your character is revealed to itself.

However, for any story—including your own—to ring true, it must resonate with something grander, with some universal theme that connects it to Everystory. The ancient Greeks understood this well, and in their dramas the characters were larger than life, wore great costumes, boots, and masks; their gestures were exaggerated, and their voices boomed loudly in the deep chasm of the open-air arenas where the dramas were held.

The roles of their characters were magnified too, because they portrayed gods, goddesses, heroes, heroines, kings, queens, princes, and princesses. Yet thousands of ordinary people thronged to see the plays, cheering and weeping in self-recognition because these productions spoke the common language of the human soul. One's personal story was somehow captured within the grand drama onstage.

The language of astrology does the same. It too encapsulates and extracts *your* story from the universal meanings embodied by those ancient gods and goddesses. It actually employs those same deities—found in the Greco-Roman pantheon of old—drawing on the myths, dramas, epics, and tales surrounding them. The attributes of these ancient deities are associated in astrology with the modern planets that bear their names.

The planets, in turn, as they move about the firmament, take on mythic scope because they—as well as the deities they are named for—symbolize archetypes. The planets of astrology are cosmic projections of the same basic life principles that the gods and goddesses represent in myths.

A JUNGIAN APPROACH

The term *archetype* means an original form, model, or ideal; another word for it could be prototype. Although the term has been in existence since Plato's time (Plato likened it to an idea in the mind of a divinity), it has been amplified considerably by the eminent psychiatrist Carl G. Jung (1875–1961) in his work on unconscious phenomena. Jung recognized the relationship between the archetypes and astrology. In his essay "On the Nature of the Psyche," for example, he stated: "The starry vault of heaven is in truth the open book of cosmic projection, in which are reflected the mythologems, i.e., the archetypes."

This book adheres to Jungian premises in its approach to archetypes, which is a psychologically oriented approach. It is also an approach that assumes that psychic life is *real*—that there is a psychic reality that is as authentic as our experience of material reality. Indeed, astrology itself operates on this premise.

According to Jung, archetypes exist in the unconscious psyche. The term *psyche* itself is indescribable; its closest definition would be "world soul." In Jung's words, the archetypes contain "everything that has ever happened on this planet since primeval times." As such, they represent humanity's accumulated experiences, repeated and reinforced over millennia. These include such basic human principles as birth, mother, father, childhood, relatedness, union, separation, death—and a legion of other experiences. Over time, these have constellated into universal themes that resonate for all people because they are common to all people, in all cultures, throughout human history.

These universal themes are embodied in mythic figures—paralleled in astrology by the planets—who serve as symbols for the archetypes. For example, each of us had a father. Our perception and experience of our father is specific since he is an actual person. Even if he disappeared before we were born, his existence still influences us.

But there is also a father archetype, an original form, model, or ideal, a prototype of father lodged in the unconscious psyche. The psyche's contents are the accumulated experience of *all* fathers throughout time, as well as a gamut of qualities, attributes, and meanings that surround this core. The expression of the father archetype, therefore, can range from the kindly, nurturing, encouraging father to the oppressive, limiting, restrictive father.

Astrology, in its process, asks: Where does *our* specific father fit within this archetype? How does he connect to the timeless human principle of father? Is he found in the story of Saturn, who, afraid they would usurp his power, devoured his children? Is he benevolent Jupiter, the inseminator, creative generator of life, affirming, generous, supportive, and exuberant? Is he Mars, the dashing warrior-lover, ready to defend his children's honor? Or is he Neptune, absent, unavailable, alcoholic—or artistic?

Perhaps he is Uranus, the ancient sky-god who thought his children ugly. They never could match his ideal; they were never good or perfect enough for him. So he suppressed them, burying them alive by pushing them back into the bowels of their mother, Mother Earth.

Our perception of our actual father, then, is mirrored somewhere in the father archetype. By finding him in the horoscope, we find the various "fathers" in our life; that is, how we project our idea of father onto others. In doing so, we learn about our relation to "father figures" in general; to outer authority, as well as to our inner authority. How do we father ourselves, for example? Do we support, affirm, and provide for our well-being? Or do we stifle or otherwise restrict our progress in life? Our story, thus, begins to unfold.

This is the process of astrology. It links ancient thinking to modern psychology. By way of the planets, the timeless myths are evoked. Their contents express, reveal, and reflect archetypal verities, eternal human themes. From these, we catch a glimpse of a larger psychic reality of which we are also a part because we share a common matrix, a world soul. Our story is connected to the story of the human family.

Astrology, then, is really a symbolic language. It is the language of the psyche in the same way that myths, dreams, fantasies, and other products of psychic life are. The planets, therefore, described in astrology in a mythic context, reflect aspects of our human psychology. As such, just as we do, they display both positive and negative sides. They are full-ranged, rich, expressive, complex, and subtle, just as we are.

A LANGUAGE OF SYMBOLS

We will explore the planets, the myths surrounding them, the life principles they embody, and their psychological applications in separate chapters of this book.

Astrology is a symbolic language—but it is also a language of symbols. As such, it makes use of pictographs, or glyphs, to depict its main vocabulary, which consists of planets, signs of the zodiac, and the horoscopic circle itself. Therefore, to make sense of the language, you need to know how to read the glyphs, which are astrology's ABCs, its visual alphabet.

In describing the planets of astrology, the circle, the crescent, and the cross are the three rudimentary components of this alphabet. The circle, O, is a symbol for "spirit," an elusive term that conjures up a kind of divine will, or animating, even activating, force in life. It is an unseen, intangible principle—yet it is part of human experience.

The crescent, ☽, is a symbol for "soul," an equally elusive term. Soul implies a kind of depth and emotional connection. Like spirit, soul is also unseen and intangible. But, unlike spirit, which seems to enter from outside a thing, soul seems to exist *in* something. In that sense, soul suggests a principle that mediates body and spirit. (The word *soul,* as used here, is not the same as psyche, although there is a close approximation.)

The cross, +, is a symbol for "matter," manifested reality. Matter has spatial and temporal dimensions, form, substance, and physicality. It is perceived and experienced through our sense organs.

In astrology each planet makes symbolic use of one, two, or three of these basic components. The glyph for the Sun, for example, (which in astrology is treated like a planet) is the circle itself, with a dot in the middle: ⊙. The Sun embodies the principle of spirit.

The glyph for the Moon (which in astrology is also considered a planet) is the crescent: ☽. The Moon embodies the principle of soul.

The glyphs for the remaining planets are:

Mercury	—	☿
Venus	—	♀
Mars	—	♂
Jupiter	—	♃
Saturn	—	♄
Uranus	—	♅
Neptune	—	♆
Pluto	—	♀

Pluto is also represented in astrology with a nontraditional glyph: ♇. This glyph stands for the initials of the astronomer, Percival Lowell, who predicted the planet's discovery.

The twelve signs of the zodiac and their glyphs are pictographs of constellations:

Aries	—	♈
Taurus	—	♉
Gemini	—	♊
Cancer	—	♋
Leo	—	♌
Virgo	—	♍
Libra	—	♎
Scorpio	—	♏
Sagittarius	—	♐
Capricorn	—	♑
Aquarius	—	♒
Pisces	—	♓

(Each of these glyphs will be discussed as they specifically apply to the meanings of the signs—and the constellations associated with them—in the general chapter on the signs.)

The horoscope itself is an astrological symbol. In the language of astrology it is the working text from which the personality is read. All the components of astrology's lexicon are contained within or around the horoscope.

In the symbolic sense, the horoscope is also a kind of *mandala,* a Sanskrit term that means "magic circle," a design motif used in Eastern art and religion to symbolize the universe. In the *mandala*'s various designs, a circle is squared or a square is encircled. Keeping in mind, then, the three components of astrology's language of symbols, the *mandala* depicts the mediation of spirit (circle) and matter (square) as an expression of soul (psyche). The horoscope is such a diagram, depicting a psychic universe. (Chapter 3 will explore the horoscope in greater detail.)

Astrology is an intuitive art and a psychological tool. But it is also a rigorous working technique. Its planets, signs, constellations, and the horoscope itself comprise its primary vocabulary—all of which will be discussed in this book. However, the more complex vocabulary of astrology's lexicon is beyond the scope of this book, as are its various advanced technical methods.

Yet, vocabulary, whether simple or advanced, is not the same as language. It takes years of training and practice to learn the intricacies of the astrological language. In fact, fluency in any language must always go beyond book-learning. In this important sense, then, this book will not make you an astrologer, but it will show you what astrology is *about*.

This is also a book for those who want to know what astrology's special gift is, that is, what it has to offer that can make a person delighted to receive it. If we really think about it, that is what a really good gift does: It has something that captivates the heart and reflects the inexpressible within us. A really good gift *recognizes* us, and that, simply stated, is what astrology does.

ABOUT THIS BOOK

The Astrology Sourcebook is divided into three parts. The first part comprises two chapters.

Chapter 1 covers the early history of astrology, tracing its beginnings to the civilizations that lined the banks of the Tigris and Euphrates Rivers in the ancient region of Mesopotamia. There, astrology was practiced by astrologer-priests skilled in divination as part of a long and sacred religious tradition.

In chapter 2, the Greek influence on Western astrology is explored. The ancient Greeks codified the system of astrology that is largely used today. They developed and expanded the use of the personal horoscope and brought their genius in geometry to astrological technique. However, they drew heavily upon Mesopotamian and ancient Egyptian traditions in developing their interpretations.

Although we also touch briefly on other astrologies in other cultures and times in chapter 2, the main thrust of this book is on the Western tradition as derived from the ancient Greeks.

Part II comprises three chapters. The first, chapter 3, describes the structure of the horoscope itself and its key components. Based mainly on the Greek model, the horoscope wheel is examined by way of the signs and houses that divide it into twelve equal segments. As a planet moves through the horoscope (a diagram of the sky), it "wears" a sign and "lives" in a house, according to the segment of sky it occupies at a given time. In this chapter, we use the Sun as an example of a planet occupying a sign and house (a segment of sky), placing it accordingly in a sample horoscope. A "real" horoscope would contain all the planets occupying a variety of signs (and houses).

In chapter 4, we trace the Sun's annual path through each of the twelve signs in greater detail, showing how the seasonal unfolding of the year resonates with the astrological meanings inherent in each sign the Sun occupies each month—beginning with the Sun in Aries in springtime and ending with the Sun in Pisces at winter's end. A full discussion of each sign and pertinent auxiliary information are also offered.

Chapter 5 is devoted to the four elements of astrology: fire, earth, air, and water. In astrology, each sign "contains" one of these elements. In this chapter, we connect astrology's elements to psychological principles largely derived from Jung's original insights into psychological types.

Part III covers the planets in astrology. The planets are the players in the astrological drama. As archetypes, or life principles common to all peoples, they represent universal truths projected as myths, stories, and legends. In each chapter, we explore these myths from the Greco-Roman perspective, since astrology's planetary figures and their meanings emanate from these myths.

Although planets symbolize particular archetypes, it is essential to understand that every planet in astrology expresses its archetypal nature in a variety of ways according to the sign it is in, its relative position to another planet, and the house it occupies.

In chapter 6, the major lights, the Sun and Moon, are discussed; the Sun stands for our self-identity and will, the Moon for our instinctual life and emotions, as well as our connection to the maternal principle.

Chapter 7 deals with the universal trickster figure, Mercury, known as Hermes to the Greeks. He personifies the intricacies of the human mind and its often cunning, always complex, shifting nature. The planet Mercury in astrology encompasses these meanings.

In chapter 8, mythological lovers Venus and Mars are paired. As planets in astrology, the signs they are in, their relative position to each other, and the houses they occupy in a horoscope indicate such things as how we express love and sexuality, whether these come easily or with difficulty, and in which setting we relate best and attract others to us.

Chapter 9 examines the motif of the father by way of the planets

Jupiter and Saturn as reflected in their respective mythologies. We explore the full range of meaning ascribed to each planet, particularly as these relate to the archetypal principles of expansion and contraction.

Finally, in chapter 10, the relatively new planets—Uranus, Neptune, and Pluto—are discussed, along with a brief history of their discoveries. Since they exist at the outer reaches of our solar system, these planets remain in a sign (or segment of sky) for long periods of time. Their impact in a horoscope is profound, both collectively and individually. Known in astrology as the "generational" planets, they reflect the zeitgeist, or spirit of an age.

PART I

Astrology's Historical Source

To study any language, it is often useful to explore its roots, its etymological core because we can discover its true sense. The meaning of the term *etymology* is precisely that: It is derived from the Greek word *etumos*, which means "true."

Similarly, by tracing astrology's origins, its earliest known use, and its primary evolution, we can learn how, when, and where its linguistic structure developed. By doing so, we may find its true sense, its etymology.

Astrology, like any other field of knowledge, is both a reflection and creation of its time and culture, shifting its primary emphasis accordingly. For example, beginning in the late nineteenth century, how people thought about themselves and the world changed radically, due in large part to the discovery—and probe—of the subconscious mind by Sigmund Freud (1856–1939) and his followers. Astrology was also influenced by the inward-looking spirit of those times, and continues to be so.

In today's world, astrology has diverged considerably from the prediction-based, often fatalistic orientation of its pre–nineteenth century past, currently aligning itself in tone and practice to advances in psychology, psychodynamics, and human relations in general—its emphasis now placed largely on such things as character analysis, self-discovery, and personal growth. And while many modern astrologers offer predictive services, they are mainly presented as trends or forecasts, not unlike a weather report, where events are subject to the uncertain winds of change.

Thus, along with the changing times, astrology has gone through *its* own inevitable changes. Yet, its basic language, as developed by its early practitioners, has remained the same. Only the meanings inherent in its vocabulary have been expanded, deepened, and enriched—necessitated by the requirements of cultural growth.

What also has remained the same is astrology's underlying principle, summed up in its simple yet timeless maxim: *as above, so below*. In fuller verse, it reads as follows:

> *Heaven above*
> *Heaven below*
> *Stars above*
> *Stars below*
> *All that is above*
> *Also is below*
> *Grasp this*
> *And rejoice.*

The precise origin of this verse is obscure. But an early Christian teacher and theologian Origen (@ A.D. 185–254) captured its spirit when he stated, "Understand that thou art a second world in miniature, and that the Sun and the Moon are within thee, and also the stars."

Today, astrologers call this same principle the "law of correspondences." That is, the macrocosm (sky) and the microcosm (events on Earth) are reflections of the same reality. One does not "cause" the other. Rather, they coincide, or "correspond" with one another, presenting parallel yet interrelated images of a similar pattern. It is the astrologer's task, then, to discern the pattern, to read and interpret it, to make it legible to others.

In the following chapters, we will review how astrologers of the past created the structure of the language, developed it, and established its lexicon—enabling astrologers today not only to read but also to reimagine those intriguing patterns that have been drawn onto the sky since the dawn of consciousness.

Astrology's Ancient Beginnings

MOST PEOPLE ARE AWARE THAT ASTROLOGY IS AN ANCIENT PRACTICE. BUT few know its history. When did it actually arise?

Certainly in its most primal sense astrology could be said to have begun the moment our earliest human ancestors stood up, lifted their heads, and gazed up at the sky, seeking to find meaning in its awesome mystery. It may have been during some prehistoric dawn as they emerged from the darkness of their caves—the Sun emerging too in a glorious blaze from the dark womb of the Earth.

Or perhaps it was later in time, during some desert twilight, when a silvery sliver of Moon peeked demurely through the clouds, like a maiden peering through her veil, a shy, crescent smile on her lips. Or when a lone morning star was seen wandering the heavens, aimless as a sheep straying from its fold. Or, more dramatically, when a comet streaked brilliantly across the sky. Or when the Sun's eclipse suddenly cast the midday world in darkness.

It could be said that astrology began at any one of those moments, or myriad others. In an early world that depended for its sheer survival on the bounty of the sky—because it brought rain, warmth, starlight and moonlight, nightfall and daylight, even thunder, lightning, shadows, and rainbows—everything revealed from above seemed to carry great meaning and portent, if only one could penetrate its secrets.

Indeed, *everything* in nature had meaning; it was alive, vibrant, powerful, teeming with movement and invisible energy, with unrelenting drive and intent. The sky too moved, its eternal display animated by the same divine, vitalized forces that drove the rest of the natural world. And like everything in nature, humankind had to discern its intentions and hidden messages in order to remain in harmony with it, and ultimately to mediate nature's overwhelming powers.

SUMERIA

There are no written records, of course, to document the precise, prehistoric moment when astrology began. But at the dawn of recorded history, in the ancient Middle Eastern city of Sumer in southern Mesopotamia, an archaic form of astrology could be textually discerned. It was in Sumer that the art of writing—in the form of cuneiform script—was invented some five thousand years ago.

In their comprehensive book *Outer Space: Myths, Name Meanings, Calendars*, Gertrude and James Jobes tell of a black stone carving unearthed from Sumer, called a *matsebah*, believed to date around 3000 B.C. On it, ten word-signs, or glyphs, were traced: a crescent, two star glyphs, an unknown form, a lamp, a fish, a fish emerging from a stream, a dog, a scorpion, and a bird. The crescent depicted the Moon; the star glyphs depicted a morning star and an evening star.

Bird, beast, fish, insect, and lamp each stood for a unique cluster of stars, a sky-picture—what we now call a constellation. Each of these glyphs also identified a god or goddess who ruled a particular sphere of human life. In this scheme, the glyphs, stars, and deities were really one and the same; a star or a cluster of stars symbolized a god or goddess. The stars, then, like the deities that were worshiped, resonated in some way with human affairs.

MESOPOTAMIA

By around 2500 B.C., extensive and more detailed written records began to appear in other early civilizations of Mesopotamia. These texts tied observed celestial events to specific omens that applied directly to human affairs.

In the ancient world of the Middle East, however, such omens were meant solely to help princes and kings rule their city-states along the Tigris and Euphrates Rivers. (These old city-states of Mesopotamia loosely comprise the modern regions of Iraq and northeast Syria.)

A typical omen of the time stated, for example, ". . . when a great star like fire rises from the east and disappears in the west, the troops of the enemy in battle will be slain . . ." Or, even more ominously, ". . . when the planet [Mars] culminates and becomes brilliant, the king will die."

The region of Mesopotamia encompassed several kingdoms and empires over a wide period of time, beginning as far back as 5000 B.C. (with a settlement at Jarmo, where the earliest known pottery was unearthed). Mesopotamia also included the Babylonian empire, which began around 2000 B.C., and was comprised of various cities, like Babylon, Ur, and Lagash.

BABYLONIA

During a later period in Mesopotamia, around 2000 B.C., an even more elaborate and detailed omen literature—based on specific sky activity—started to appear more regularly, originating in Babylonia in the lower Euphrates valley. Written on clay tablets in cuneiform text, an ongoing work called *Enuma Anu Enlil* (names of sky-gods) was initiated there and developed. On the tablets, omens were systematically collected, categorized, cataloged, and codified to match up with eclipses, Moon phases, simple planetary movements, and the like.

Once classified, these omens were assigned to four deities: Sun, Moon, Venus (who the Babylonians called Ishtar), and a weather god, Adad, who ruled such things as thunder, lightning, and cloud formations.

By around 1000 B.C., the final codification of omens in the *Enuma Anu Enlil* was completed, although not all the tablets have survived. What has survived has mostly been unearthed from the library of a seventh-century B.C. Assyrian king named Ashurbanipal. During a relatively short period of Assyrian ascendancy in Mesopotamia, he managed to gather up and make copies of several texts from old Babylonian sites and temples.

Another set of cuneiform tablets from King Ashurbanipal's library, known as the *Ammizaduga* tablets, describe the risings, settings, and other movements of the planet Venus—revered in Babylonia as the "mistress of heaven" as she regally spanned the sky. Omens were ascribed to Venus's proximity to various stars—but especially to the Moon. (Since the Sun and

Moon were regarded as deities, they are here capitalized. This convention has persisted in astrology and will be adhered to throughout this book.)

The Moon, depicted as a bearded, masculine god traveling about the sky in a crescent-shaped boat, was considered to be more significant than the Sun, and was much more closely observed. It was the Moon, for example, that shifted its shape by waxing and waning. It also moved in so many unexpected ways, whereas the Sun was steady, constant, dependable—thus not apt to signify anything sudden or portentous.

It was the Moon too that seemed rhythmically connected to women's mysteries and the watery pull of the tides; thus, its effect on the deeper layers of nature was almost palpable. As a result the Moon was watched most carefully by Babylonian astrologers for significant natural events, especially around lunar (Moon) eclipses. A typical omen, for example, stated, ". . . when the Moon is eclipsed, there will be flood and the produce of the waters of the land will be abundant . . ."

The Sun, who ruled the seasons, was believed to be the Moon's daughter (or son, depending on the region). Venus, as mediator between the two—she was seen to travel from one to the other—was a kind of sister-star to the Moon. So Venus's proximity to the Sun or Moon was closely watched for significant meanings. When Venus rose before the Sun, for example—as a morning star—she was said to bring splendor, fertility, and prosperity to the land.

The sumptuous delights of Venus as she rose before dawn are beautifully captured in an excerpt from *Hymn to Ishtar*, found in J. B. Pritchard's book *Ancient Near Eastern Texts Relating to the Old Testament*:

> Ishtar is clothed with pleasure and love.
> She is laden with vitality, charm, and voluptuousness.
> In lips she is sweet; life is in her mouth.

At her appearance rejoicing becomes full.
She is glorious; veils are thrown over her head.
Her figure is beautiful; her eyes are brilliant.

We will discuss Venus, her mythology, and her meaning in astrology in chapter 8's section on the planets.

CHALDEA

The Chaldeans, a Semitic people, inhabited the southern part of Babylonia. They are particularly credited with major advances in astrology. Their astrologers were assiduous observers, were highly skilled in mathematics, and kept detailed records of sky phenomena. Indeed, the Chaldeans are said to have constructed the first known star-charts around 700 B.C.

By consulting such charts, which were drawn up continuously over hundreds of years, the Chaldeans could discern a distinct, recognizable, *recurring* pattern in the wanderings of the five visible planets (those we know today as Mercury, Venus, Mars, Jupiter, and Saturn). Each planet, they noted, had a cycle, as they returned to the same place in the sky after a specific period of time.

This discovery was useful for the astrologers' duties of timing festivals, offerings, religious rites, and temple ceremonies regularly held in honor of a god or goddess who ruled a particular planet. (As interpreters of divine intentions, astrologers of the time had a priestly role.)

Most important, however, with the knowledge of recurring planetary cycles, the astrologer-priests of Chaldea held the key to *future* celestial events—events that they could now reliably foretell, along with corresponding long-term predictions of interest to the king (his tenure, for example), the populace he ruled (events such as floods, feast or famine, plagues), and the kingdom's security (matters of war and peace).

By the end of the fourth century B.C., the Chaldeans had compiled numerous written tables of both lunar and planetary movement. These detailed records could be called the prototypes of the future ephemerides, books that keep track of the daily positions of the Sun, Moon, and planets, so useful to later astrologers.

The word *ephemeris* derives from the Latin word for diary, which in turn comes from the Greek word for daily, or "on the day." The ephemeris is an essential tool for constructing a personal horoscope, since the positions of all the planets at a person's birth must be calculated for this purpose. The first printed ephemeris was called the *Kalendarium Novum*, which covered the years 1474 to 1506, and was calculated by Regiomontanus, a German mathematician-astrologer and his teacher Johannes Peuerbach.

The ephemeris is virtually the modern astrologer's bible. (Indeed, no self-respecting astrologer would leave home without it!) With the ephemeris, the astrologer compares the positions of planets at a person's date of birth with the positions of planets at a later date, a procedure essential for evaluating a person's life situation for any given time.

THE DISCOVERY OF THE ZODIAC

In their celestial observations, the Chaldean astrologers noticed something else of significance: The planets, in their wanderings against the backdrop of stars, seemed to move in roughly the same plane. This kept all the planets tied—literally, like a belt—to a certain region of the sky. With this discovery, the Chaldeans also noticed that the quick-moving Moon regularly passed through twelve principal star-clusters, or constellations, on this belt. Each constellation was designated by a sign, named for the constellation.

The Chaldeans did not develop this major finding any further astrologically—except for calling the belt of twelve constellations *The Road of Life*. What they observed, measured, and recorded, however, was the zodiac, the basic, structural form of classical—and modern—astrology. The zodiac set the stage for the horoscope (developed later by the Greeks), which positioned all the planets around the circle of the zodiac for a specific time and place.

The Chaldeans' great legacy, however, was not limited to the zodiac, record keeping, and keen sky watching, which made them astronomers. It was their highly developed gifts of prophecy as well, putting *human* relevance into following the stars, which made them astrologers.

They used science and art to divine the patterns of the sky, applying these to earthly matters in their own mystic fashion. Perhaps underscoring this, to this very day the word *Chaldean* has come to mean someone versed in occult learning: an astrologer, numerologist, soothsayer, magician.

Indeed, in our modern age—even among those who are not astrologers —we can still find traces of the Chaldean legacy because we have not really lost the urge to connect to the sky, speak to it, and listen for what it may have to say to us. We still "thank our lucky stars," for example, when we survive a danger; and children still wish on stars. Farmers and gardeners often still plant by the Moon, just as lovers and others gaze longingly at it, weaving hopes and spinning dreams from its magnetic light.

In addition, the enormous popularity of science fiction, the slew of movies, books, television shows, and magazines dealing with aliens, and the broad appeal of the modern space program itself all attest to our unceasing fascination with "life out there," and our yearning to make contact with it.

Moreover, each time we look up devotedly in prayer toward heaven, we continue to invoke the Chaldean heritage: the belief in the sky as the dwelling place of God. It is, of course, a heritage as old as human history itself. It has simply been upheld, preserved, and passed down—across cultures and through the ages—from the ancient ziggurats, or watchtowers, of the old Chaldean astrologer-priests.

from East to West:

Astrology's Winding Path Through Time and Place

THE GREEKS

Although the ancient Greeks are largely credited with the development
of astrology as we know it today, it was not really indigenous to their
culture; they essentially had to import it. It was actually a Chaldean
astrologer-priest—a man named Berossus—who brought astrology to the
Greeks from across the sea. Berossus opened a school of astrology early in
the third century B.C. on the Aegean island of Kos. At the time, the Greeks
had no astrology of their own.

Kos was also home to a medical school (Hippocrates, the "Father of
Medicine," was born there). Although astrology and medicine had earlier
been linked in Mesopotamia, on Kos they made an even stronger connection. It was in a Hippocratic medical work, "On Diets," that Babylonian
astrology was first mentioned in the Greek language.

To this day, astrology adheres to the medical tradition developed on Kos because every part of the human body—from the head to the feet—is assigned to an astrological sign. (In our later discussion of signs in chapter 4, we will indicate what the specific matchups are and how they correspond in meaning.)

Babylonian astrology eventually came to the Greeks on a more massive scale, with the wide-ranging conquests of Alexander the Great (356–323 B.C.), the legendary Macedonian general whose armies swept over Greece, Egypt, Persia (modern Iran), Afghanistan, and parts of India, as well as the entire region of Mesopotamia.

As a result of one of Alexander's greatest goals—to fuse the East and West—the Greek, Egyptian, and Oriental worlds freely infiltrated each culture. Yet, Alexander's most enduring achievement was to extend Greek influence to a vast area of the ancient world, ushering in the Hellenistic era (the dominance of Greek language, culture, and civilization) of the next few hundred years.

And, in a kind of reverse trend, Babylonian astrology found a rich and fertile soil in Greece itself, where it flourished. Greek, in turn, became the language of the conquered lands, affecting how Babylonian astrology was translated—and ultimately reformulated.

ANCIENT EGYPT

By indirect way of Alexander's conquests, Babylonian astrology was also transmitted into Egypt, but its effect was blurred by Greek developments in astrology, which increasingly prevailed. Before Alexander, however, Egypt had its own astrological tradition, which was comingled with a highly mystical belief system that centered around Ra, the Sun-god.

For the Egyptians, it was the Sun-god, not the Moon-god, who traveled by boat through the sky—above by day, and below by night. When the Sun's boat sank into the western horizon every night, it was said to be met by a serpent or dragon, which threatened to destroy the Sun. The Egyptian god Set then had the task of repelling this demon so that the Sun might safely cross the entire underworld at night and be reborn at dawn.

In this same way, a person might survive death itself and be reborn, with divine help, mediation, and proper ritual, especially by preparing adequately for the night journey after death—provisions and all. Indeed, human life was said to mirror the Sun's path, the underworld (death) serving as an extension, or continuation, of the upper world (life).

In keeping with their emphasis on the Sun's preeminence, the Egyptians also inaugurated the solar (Sun-based) calendar year of 365 days, thus relegating the Moon to a more subsidiary role in human affairs. (The calendar developed in Mesopotamia was Moon-based: twelve monthly Moon-cycles to a year, with a thirteenth Moon-cycle occasionally added.)

The Sun's dominance over the Moon was reflected in Egyptian mythology, where the Sun could actually assign responsibility for the Moon to another god—in this case, to Thoth, the god of mental skills, writing, letters, literature, language, poetry, and numbers. Thoth became a kind of delegate for the Sun, and, as the Sun's virtual messenger, he served the other deities (planets) as well.

Thoth represents an early version of astrology's Mercury, who is known today as the messenger god, scurrying to and fro on his winged feet. (We will discuss Mercury, his mythology, and his various meanings in astrology in chapter 7, in the section on the planets.)

Central to Egypt's prosperity was the yearly flooding of the Nile, which inundated the otherwise dry desert soil along its banks. Because of this phenomenon, the so-called Dog Star, Sirius, was carefully observed by the early Egyptians, since at the summer solstice (when Sirius rose at dawn in the ancient capital of Memphis), the Nile flooded the countryside, bringing renewed fertility to the land. The dog days of summer signaled a time when Sirius added its bright glow to the Sun's already powerful, life-generating heat.

ALEXANDRIAN EGYPT

With Alexander's conquests, it was the new Greek astrology that now flooded over Egypt—albeit with Babylonian undercurrents—creating a fertile soil in the *new* Egyptian capital, Alexandria (founded by Alexander in 332 B.C.), and ruled by the Macedonian kings, called the Ptolemies.

An enormous treasure of occult literature, known as the Hermetic writings (the Greek god Hermes now replacing Thoth), soon emerged in Alexandria, all written in Greek. These works covered a vast array of arcane subjects, including astrology, alchemy, and magic. Around 160 B.C., a popular textbook on astrology—possibly the first—also appeared and was attributed to an Egyptian priest of earlier times, Petosiris, addressing a king named Nechepso. Its influence was far-reaching because it laid down technical rules derived from ancient Babylonian sources.

Astrology was on the rise all over the Hellenistic world (Greece and the conquered lands that ranged from Egypt all the way across Persia to Central Asia, and as far as northern India) but especially in Alexandria. In those heady times of Greek cultural expansion, Alexandria flourished as *the* great intellectual center for Greek learning and, in particular, for the "new" Greek astrology. It was an astrology mostly inspired by esoteric knowledge culled from the Middle East and comingled with Egyptian thought—but also enriched by the Greek genius for philosophy and geometry.

PTOLEMY

In keeping with their traditional musings on such themes as the nature of the universe itself, the Greeks began to envision the sky as the cosmos—that is, as an orderly and harmonious whole, a sacred universe of which Earth was an intricate part. And, to their rational way of thinking, the cosmos had a schematic, geometric design.

In the year A.D. 150, Claudius Ptolemy, a Greek living in Alexandria, devised a theory of the cosmos, which put Earth at the center of the universe—a belief that continued to hold in all of Europe until the sixteenth century, when Copernicus posited a Sun-centered system. Ptolemy was an astronomer and an astrologer. Indeed, these disciplines were considered one and the same (called *astrologia*) until Copernicus's time.

Although abstract and conceptual, Ptolemy's scheme of the cosmos is really empirically based. It derives from the direct, natural, sense-experience a person standing on our planet has of the sky. We perceive the Sun, for example, as moving *up* from the horizon and sinking *down* into it, thus circling over us. This image is deeply etched in our visual memory; it informs our sense of reality.

Copernicus's discovery taught us that what we experience as *real* is not necessarily *true*—that our senses often lie to us. The Sun does not circle around us. It is *we* who are tethered to the Sun.

Astrologers understand this paradox. Astrology, however, still adheres to Ptolemy in that its point of view is geocentric, or Earth-centered.

Astrology works with the human perspective from Planet Earth. In doing so, it psychologically validates our perception of reality as we contemplate the sky. It acknowledges what we might call our "soul-knowledge."

Ptolemy authored four astrological treatises, the *Tetrabiblos*, as well as an astronomical work, the *Almagest* (in which, among other things, he published the first star-catalog, expanded from the Chaldean star-charts, listing 1,022 stars, arranged by constellations). In the *Tetrabiblos*, the meanings of the signs of the zodiac, the planets, and other key astrological principles were set down in a way that is still applicable today. (However, many of Ptolemy's astrological precepts have fallen into disuse.)

It was Ptolemy who enlarged on the technique of "aspects" in astrology, which is essential to all interpretative work. Aspects are the geometric angles, expressed in degrees of celestial longitude—that planets make to each other—as viewed from Earth. Ptolemy posited that this geometry of the planets led to a "mingling of their dispositions" in specific ways. The nature of one planet, he stated, when combined with another, forms a result that includes both their meanings.

The Greeks considered five planetary angles to be significant. Known today as the Ptolemaic aspects, they are as follows, with their respective astrological glyphs included:

Conjunction	= ☌ =	planets are 0 degrees apart
Sextile	= ✶ =	planets are 60 degrees apart
Square	= □ =	planets are 90 degrees apart
Trine	= △ =	planets are 120 degrees apart
Opposition	= ☍ =	planets are 180 degrees apart

A simplified way to envision aspects for our purposes is to imagine the geometric angles made by the hands of a circular wall clock—with each hand pointing to the position of a planet around the circumference of the clock.

When both hands are on twelve, for example, two planets (Jupiter, ♃, and Venus, ♀, for example) are in a conjunction, ☌, or 0 degrees apart, as illustrated (Fig. 1).

If one hand is on twelve and the other on two, the angle formed is 60 degrees apart, a sextile, ✶, as illustrated (Fig. 2).

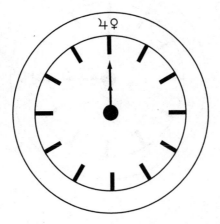

FIGURE I

FIGURE 2

If the other hand is on three, the angle formed is 90 degrees apart, a square, □, as illustrated (Fig. 3).

On four, the angle formed is 120 degrees apart, a trine, △, as illustrated (Fig. 4).

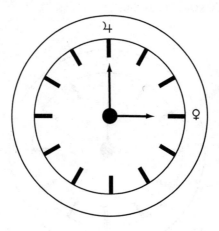

FIGURE 3

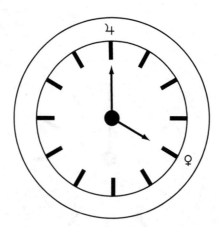

FIGURE 4

When the hands are opposite one another, they are 180 degrees apart, an opposition, ☍, as illustrated (Fig. 5).

FIGURE 5

With the use of aspects, a complex language of astrology is created, since, by combining planetary symbolisms, a meaningful astrological sentence can be constructed. (The planets and their relative positions "on the wall clock" will vary, but their aspects are always described in accordance with their angular relation to each other.)

Following is a simple example of an astrological sentence: If the planet Jupiter (who in Ptolemy's time was said to be "good," bringing expansion) makes a conjunction with the planet Venus, love (Venus's realm) is increased. If the planet Saturn (who, in Ptolemy's time was said to be "bad," bringing restriction), however, makes a conjunction with Venus, love is limited, or decreased.

It is more complicated, however, if Jupiter and Venus form a square or opposition; then it is difficult to integrate their natures, since these aspects are considered "hard" or "difficult." And, if Saturn and Venus form a sextile or a trine, it is easy to integrate their qualities, since these aspects are considered "soft" or "easy."

In astrology, the Ptolemaic aspects are still paramount, although many other aspects, hard and soft, have been added to the mix.

Ptolemy also gathered together the findings of other astrologers—dating as far back as the Chaldeans—and included them in his work. This comprehensive act of his preserved an entire body of ancient astrological knowledge for future generations.

THE ROMANS

Although Ptolemy belonged to the Greek intellectual and cultural life of Alexandria, the city itself belonged in his time to the new conquerors, the Romans. Greek astrology had already permeated Roman society, however, among the masses and the elite. A Roman emperor of Ptolemy's time, Hadrian, was a practicing astrologer, as later was Tiberius. Court astrologers were also commonplace throughout the Roman empire.

Even earlier, during Rome's golden age (the reign of Augustus Octavian, 27 B.C.–A.D. 14), Greek astrology was fully absorbed into Roman society. It was during this period that the Latin poet Manilius wrote his great multivolume literary work on the stars, *Astronomica*—essentially a textbook on astrology written in verse.

In the fourth century, another Latin author, Firmicus Maternus, wrote *Matheseos libri* (*Books on Astrology*), which widely influenced scholars and intellectuals of old Rome. Still, the bulk of astrological writings in the Roman world, including Ptolemy's works and that of his contemporary Vettius Valens, were not only written in Greek but also came from Greek sources.

The immediate centuries following Ptolemy, however, saw the once-powerful Roman empire crumble, its final demise coming with the Goths' sack of Rome in A.D. 410. With this, the age of antiquity drew to a close—along with its pagan deities, as a nascent Christianity was also taking hold in Europe. By the sixth century, astrology had virtually disappeared there, as had all Greek learning and culture.

BYZANTIUM

There were really two "Romes" in the Roman empire. The other one, called Constantinople, was on the Greek Hellespont, where Istanbul now stands. Established in the year A.D. 330 by the Christianized Roman emperor, Constantine the Great, it was originally the eastern wing of the Roman empire. After the fall of Rome, however, Constantinople survived for a thousand years as the capital of what was known as the Byzantine Empire.

In Constantinople, Greek astrological writings were preserved, for Greek was still the city's official language, as well as in the eastern regions in general. By the eighth century, however, the Byzantine Empire had also dwindled, especially as the Islamic conquests swept over the Middle East and North Africa, areas that were part of Byzantium.

These areas comprised old Mesopotamia and Egypt. Ancient Greek astrological manuscripts were uncovered there (especially in Alexandria), and transported to new Islamic cultural centers such as Damascus, Baghdad, and Cairo for translation into Arabic. Finally, in the ninth century, as part of a peace treaty the ruler of Constantinople turned over to the caliph of Baghdad the city's entire store of Greek writings, including the works of Ptolemy.

ARABIC ASTROLOGY

Greek astrology, now translated into Arabic, found a new home in the Islamic lands, where it again flourished. The imaginative symbolism of astrology was highly compatible with the Islamic affinity for allegory and abstract imagery, as well as with the flowery, poetic Arabic language. Astrology also lent itself easily to the region's timeless desert skill—navigating by the stars. Additionally, the Greek love of geometry was matched in kind by the Arabic love of numbers. (Indeed, the Arabs combined numbers *and* geometry to create algebra.) Greek astrology, then, with its mix of geometry, numbers, and metaphor, had immediate appeal in Islamic culture.

Arabic astrologers brought numerous innovations and additions to the Greek material, especially in their emphasis on such (still much-used) techniques as electional astrology, where a most propitious time is found for an upcoming event; and horary astrology, which spells out an answer to a specific question based on an astrological chart for the moment of inquiry.

Thus, by an ironic twist of history, Greek astrology was revived and revitalized at its very place of origin, Mesopotamia—a land now converted to Islam. And by yet another historical twist, the work of a great ninth-century Islamic astrologer Abû Ma'shar found its way into Moorish Spain and Sicily three or four centuries later, where it was translated into Latin.

With this, Europe was in possession—once again—of Greek-inspired astrology!

ASTROLOGY'S RETURN TO EUROPE

By the thirteenth century, almost all the Greek astrology that had passed through the Islamic world was once more in the hands of Latin-speaking Europe. In Italy, court astrologers were in vogue again, and *astrologia* was taught at the universities. And by the sixteenth century, with the renewal of interest in antiquity brought on by the Renaissance, full-blown Greek astrology, in its final Latinized form (and with its Islamic enhancements) was again flourishing in Europe. Astrology had come full circle on its winding path through time and place.

But the circle was broken again by the sheer force of the scientific revolution only a century later because the new Sun-centered worldview posited by Copernicus had by now firmly taken hold, and astrology could find no place in this new order. The theoretical schism between the Ptolemaic and Copernican systems was now final and irrevocable. Astronomy and astrology could not be reconciled, although such astronomers as Tycho Brahe, Johannes Kepler, and Galileo stayed attuned to astrology. Indeed, Kepler valiantly tried to integrate astrology into the Copernican system but failed.

WHICH BRINGS US FULL CIRCLE

From the seventeenth century to the present day, astrology has followed a jagged, eccentric, and irregular path—like the very planets it charts. And like those planets, from time to time it has seemed to stop short in its tracks, to abruptly change its course and retrograde backward. At other times, astrology has seemed to vanish completely below the horizon. And, at still other times, it has seemed to rise like the morning Sun, filled with the promise of a new day.

Today, astrology is alive and well and living in all corners of the globe. It has also branched out in all directions, finding new adherents from a wide range of disciplines. And while the central approach of this particular book is psychological, astrology has also been well applied to such fields as health and alternative medicine, agriculture, and gardening, as well as weather, geological, and earthquake studies.

An active branch of modern astrology, called mundane astrology, engages itself with world events, national leaders, royalty, governments, nations and the like, and with historical periods and cycles in general. In financial astrology, stock market and business trends, global monetary practices, and the price of gold are analyzed.

Sophisticated techniques and "schools" have also evolved in astrology, such as Uranian astrology and cosmobiology, both of which provide useful methods for such predictive-type work as timing and forecasting, as well as for precise, detailed analyses of personal histories and events.

OTHER ASTROLOGICAL TRADITIONS

The focus of this book is primarily on Western astrology, mainly as it has come down to us from the Greeks and is practiced today. Thus, as part of Western astrology's historical tradition, its orientation and the meanings derived from it are mostly based on how life was experienced as the seasons unfolded in the northern latitudes—specifically, in Europe of the Middle Ages, when astrology was further refined from its Greek sources.

In other traditions, a rich store of astrological knowledge most emphatically exists, but it is beyond the scope of this book. However, it is certainly instructive for the sake of greater inclusiveness to survey briefly a few other (but by no means complete) significant astrological traditions.

Chinese Astrology

According to Chinese legend, when the Lord Buddha was ready to leave this world he invited all the animals to come to say good-bye, but only twelve showed up. As a result, he named a year after each one: rat, ox, tiger, rabbit, dragon, snake, horse, sheep, monkey, rooster, dog, and pig. In Chinese astrology, each animal's inherent characteristics are said to influence a person born in the year the animal rules. The hour a person is born further affects how these attributes are expressed.

Other factors, such as the birth month; the Chinese elements of water, wood, fire, earth, and metal (each ruled by a planet); and the position of the Moon are also taken into account. Five flavors (sour, salty, acrid, bitter, and sweet) and five colors (green, yellow, scarlet, white, and black) are also considered when delineating a horoscope. In addition, *yin* (receptive) and *yang* (active) energies are believed to be the twofold way of knowing the essence of all things.

The lunar calendar forms the basis of ancient Chinese astrology, the first one dating back to 2637 B.C. The early Chinese believed that the heavens reflected life on Earth very much the way a mirror does, and astrologers were expected to observe the sky carefully to describe events and foretell divine intentions. Such sky phenomena as eclipses, lightning, and even a shooting star revealed prophetic information about the course of human life below.

There is inconclusive evidence that later Chinese astrology, certainly by the third century B.C., was influenced by contact with Hellenistic astrology, possibly by way of Persia or India.

The Astrology of the Ancient Mayans
of Central America

From the second to the tenth century, Mayan civilization flowered, cover-
ing an area that encompassed Mexico's Yucatan peninsula, as well as what
is now Guatemala, Belize, and parts of El Salvador and Honduras. The
Mayans had an advanced, well-organized, and complex culture. Yet, for
unknown reasons, by the tenth century they left their great cities and dis-
persed into the surrounding jungles. Their astrological legacy, however—
preserved in several archaeological sites and museum depositories—
is enormous.

The Mayans were deeply preoccupied with keeping track of time and
interweaving celestial cycles, practices which were tied in with the gov-
erning of their fate as a people. They took special notice of Venus's risings and settings and the Moon's eclipses, which augured for good or bad
by means of an intricate and sacred (and as yet not fully understood) system of counting and calendarizing. Since Venus was envisioned as a god
whose cyclical appearance in the sky was seen to mesh with the Sun, the
planet was scrupulously observed from Mayan observatories and its
movements tabulated by astrologers for purposes of divination. The
Mayans built towering, pyramidlike structures, with radial, terraced platforms reached by steps. The platforms were designed to mark off significant seasonal points, such as solstices and equinoxes. Temples were also
positioned atop these platforms. At one famous archaeological site in the
Yucatan, Chichén Itzá, a tall, round building called the Caracol exists and
is believed by most scholars to be an observatory. Windows that open
onto the spiral stair inside its dome seem to be aligned for optimal celestial sightings.

Astrology in ancient Mayan culture embraced religion, astronomy, calendar keeping, history (which was perceived as cyclical, like heavenly events), medicine, and prophecy. Even today, in many Mayan villages so-called calendar-priests, reminiscent of the early astrologers, still perform sacred functions, as they use their ancient knowledge to treat various illnesses of body and spirit.

Hindu (Vedic) Astrology

The astrology of ancient India, still practiced today, is known as *Jyotish*. It has its roots in sacred Sanskrit texts that form the basis of the Hindu religion, called the Vedas (*Veda* means "knowledge"). This knowledge was said to be transmitted by seers (at first orally, then written down by priests around 1400 B.C.) by way of divine revelation from the shining light of the stars and planets themselves.

Contained in the Vedas (in the form of poems, sagas, hymns, and sacred incantations) are such fundamental Hindu concepts as the societal caste system, the doctrine of transmigration of souls or reincarnation, and the law of karma, where actions and deeds of one lifetime affect future lifetimes. These principles form the spiritual underpinnings of Vedic astrology.

Jyotish is predominantly a Moon-oriented system. It makes use of lunar mansions, which are twenty-eight significant degree points of the Moon's monthly path around the zodiac. It also places paramount importance on two additional powerful points in the horoscope, known as the nodes of the Moon, which play a key role in eclipses. (Nodes are used in Western astrology as well.)

Vedic astrology is rich in substance and methodology. It recognizes such things as planetary combinations, called *yogas* (*yoga* means "union," or "yoke"), which reflect karmic patterns. It also places great importance on specific time periods in one's life that coincide with certain planetary cycles called *dasas*.

Jyotish is much more integrated into Indian society than astrology is in the West. To this day, for example, it is not uncommon in India for a prospective bride and groom to have their horoscopes compared for compatibility before the marriage is approved by the couple's families.

CONCLUSION

Astrology's history is textured, varied, and interwoven with time and place, as well as culture. Yet, no matter how far astrology has traveled through time, or from which places it has come, or the cultural byways it has taken along the way, it has never really strayed from the age-old "road of life," the eternal path of the Sun, Moon, and planets around the zodiac.

Part II will explore that road—and the twelve signs of the zodiac encountered on our journey.

PART II

The Horoscope,

The Signs of the Zodiac, and

The Elements in Astrology

THE EARLIEST BABYLONIAN HOROSCOPE IS DATED 410 B.C., BUT LITTLE IS
known of its purpose. What *is* known about early horoscopes comes mostly
from the Hellenistic Greeks, who made widespread use of them. Indeed,
most of the ancient horoscopes preserved in the West are of Greek origin.

In developing the horoscope from its Mesopotamian sources, however,
the Greeks remained faithful to their individualistic and democratic traditions. To the Greek way of thinking, everyone—regardless of station in
life—had an individual, singular destiny, uniquely his or her own. A horoscope, drawn up for a person's time of birth, could reflect that uniqueness.
To the Greeks, astrology was not an exclusive, royal prerogative. It was
available to everyone.

The word *horoscope* comes from the Greek word *horoscopus*, which
means "I watch the hour." The Greeks were actually watching the constellation that was rising on the eastern horizon at a particular hour—

specifically, the hour of a person's birth. Since each constellation is designated by a sign name, what was watched became known as the rising sign, what astrologers also call the Ascendant.

The Ascendant in astrology signifies the physical body itself, a kind of first manifestation of material life. By way of the sign it is in, it also describes how someone perceives and then expresses herself or himself in the world. In psychological terms it is the persona, or mask, of the personality—the face, dress, and style a person exhibits.

Another key innovation the Greeks made was to divide the horoscope into a fixed geometric scheme. They took the zodiac (the Chaldean belt of constellations, the sky-pictures) and divided it into twelve *equal* thirty-degree segments. Each segment defined a constellation, its sign name, and a "house." Each house, in turn, stood for one of twelve arenas of life, such as money, children, work, and other categories. A house (and its corresponding sign) also had a planet "ruling" it—in the form of the god or goddess for which the planet was named. An organized system of astrology was now put in place.

The scheme of the Greek horoscope, as outlined, was actually a radical step for astrology because it began the process of lifting astrology into the symbolic sphere: It became abstract, geometric, and conceptual. By devising the horoscope as a kind of diagram, the Greeks effectively gave greater relevance to signs and houses than real constellations over the course of time. After all, a thirty-degree segment (comprising a sign and a house) does not exactly mesh with an observable constellation. How could it? A constellation varies in size; it does not come in neat, thirty-degree packets.

Actually, when the Greeks were developing the horoscope, the constellations and the signs they were named for *did* coincide—more or less.

However, because of a phenomenon called precession, which is caused by the Earth's slight wobble as it spins, the signs used in astrology and the constellations they are named for do not completely overlap today. They are "off" by some twenty-three degrees, almost a full sign.

For example, even if the Sun were traveling in the constellation of Pisces on the day you were born on April 1, for instance, your horoscope will designate you an Aries. (No, this is not an April Fool's joke!) Because of precession, the constellations and the signs named for them in the horoscope no longer match up.

It is a mistaken belief, however, among some commentators that modern astrologers are not aware of precession. Not only are astrologers keenly aware of it, but there is also an entire branch of astrology devoted to it, called sidereal astrology, which corrects for precession. (*Sidereal* means pertaining to the stars, that is, the constellations, which are simply clusters of stars forming imaginary pictures.) Sidereal astrology forms the basis of the Vedic astrology of India, outlined in the preceding chapter; there are also many Western adherents to Vedic astrology.

The type of astrology predominantly practiced in the West today, however—and the astrology addressed in this book—is called tropical astrology, as distinct from sidereal astrology. Tropical astrology is based solely on the signs of the zodiac. The constellations they once overlapped with still apply, however, as symbolic backdrops.

Tropical astrology's underlying structure is not built on the constellations but on the four seasons. Each season begins at a "turning point" of the Sun during the year: the spring equinox, the summer solstice, the fall equinox, and the winter solstice. Every spring, around March 21, when the Sun crosses the equator going north, at the spring equinox, the sign of Aries begins in astrology.

The Sun's northernmost point, the summer solstice, marks the sign of Cancer, around June 21. The sign of Libra, around September 22, begins when the Sun crosses the equator going south, at the fall equinox. And the Sun's southernmost point, the winter solstice, marks the sign of Capricorn, around December 21.

In the following chapter we describe the horoscope of tropical astrology in greater detail, with its special emphasis on the signs of the zodiac. This is followed, in chapter 4, by an overall discussion of each sign—based on the Sun's yearly travel through each of the twelve signs of the zodiac. Houses and constellations are also included in the discussion. A separate chapter is devoted to the four elements in astrology (fire, earth, air, and water) and their special use.

The components of the Horoscope:

An Astrological Primer

PLANETS, SIGNS, AND HOUSES

The main vocabulary of astrology consists of planets, signs, and houses. These three factors make up the basic syntax of a simple astrological sentence. (As we have already seen, the Ptolemaic aspects—the geometry of the planets—adds some complexity to the sentence.)

A planet is like a verb in grammar. It acts, does, is; it expresses an occurrence, state of being, or life principle. A sign describes how the planet behaves; it is like an adverb; it modifies the verb. If the planet Venus, for example, means "to love," the sign that Venus is in at a particular time (as indicated in a horoscope) describes *how* a person expresses that love.

Let us say, for example, that *your* birth horoscope has Venus in the sign of Aries. This means you express love (Venus) assertively (Aries), since Aries is a sign standing for self-assertion.

You are always the pronoun—the subject—in astrology. It is *your* Sun, *your* Venus, *your* Mars, etc., being expressed, based on your horoscope. However, a verb usually has an object—a place, person, or thing on which you project the action of the verb and its adverb. In astrology, the house that one of your planets is in at a particular time is *where* the action takes place. It is the object.

If your horoscope, for example, has Venus in Aries in the fifth house (the house of children, among other things), you express love (Venus) assertively (Aries) toward your children (fifth house).

Planet, sign, and house make up the simple beginning sentence of your complicated story. This very beginning—told by way of the horoscope—is the subject of this chapter. We will use the Sun, however (not Venus), as the example planet to illustrate the horoscope's basic structure. In chapter 4, we take the Sun through all twelve signs of the zodiac, along with the twelve houses, giving specific meanings for each sign and house.

"WHAT'S YOUR SIGN?"

There is hardly a person in this day and age who cannot readily answer the above question. Certainly, those who follow astrology in books, newspaper columns, and magazines know what sign they are. Indeed, for many such people, their astrological sign is a kind of vital statistic, a tacit piece of personal ID. But even those not versed in astrology, indifferent to it, or downright skeptical toward it will have gleaned this intriguing bit of data about themselves somewhere along the way.

But what does it mean, exactly, to say you are a particular sign? From the astrologer's point of view it means, first of all, that you respond to life in a certain way. It may mean that you tend to initiate things, for example, but you do not necessarily follow through. Or that you dislike change, preferring to maintain the status quo, and are, therefore, often hard to budge. Or, quite the contrary, that you like change and variety, constantly shifting your point of view, or perhaps moving from place to place or job to job.

Your sign will also tell the astrologer what motivates you. Is it love? Money? Sex? Family? Career? All of the above? Of course! But the astrologer looks for a dominant pattern that shapes your life choices. Your sign provides insight into what that pattern might be. And it also tells the astrologer what set of traits make up, or support, the pattern.

In knowing your sign, the astrologer actually considers many factors—besides those just mentioned—all of which combine to form a picture of the real you. The signs, with their variety of colorations, textures, and shadings, provide an especially rich palette for the astrologer's interpretive paint box.

Something else, however, is also being described when you say you *are* a particular sign. To the astrologer, you are also saying that the Sun was located in a specific place on its path along the zodiac on the day you were born. That specific place is designated by an astrological sign. Your Sun was *in* Virgo, for example, if you were born between August 22 and September 22, making you a "Virgo"; *in* Scorpio if you were born between October 23 and November 22, making you a "Scorpio," and so on.

What you know as your sign, therefore, is really only your "Sun-sign," the sign of the zodiac the Sun was in at your birth. (The planet Venus, for example, may have been in a different sign at your birth, in accordance with *its* position along the zodiac. Each of the other planets, including the Moon, would also be placed in its proper sign in your birth horoscope.)

To understand what is meant by your Sun being "placed" in a sign, an example horoscope—fashioned after the scheme developed by the Greeks

—is provided on the following page. The twelve signs of the zodiac are indicated, both in words and with their glyphs. We will explain the horoscope's basic construction before placing the Sun (in your particular Sun-sign) in the example horoscope.

It should be noted, however, that the example horoscope does *not* represent *your* personal horoscope or the horoscope of any specific individual. It is simply an instructional aid to help you understand the underlying basis of *every* horoscope. We will describe the horoscope's general structure and how its main components—planets, signs, and houses (using the Sun as the example planet)—fit into its design.

THE FOUR ANGLES OF THE HOROSCOPE

In studying the example horoscope, note that each sign is "sliced" equally, like a pizza pie; a circle encompasses all twelve signs (Fig. 6). Each of the twelve signs, in turn, comprises thirty degrees of the circle.

You will also notice that the Ascendant overlaps with the sign of Aries—the first sign of the zodiac, the starting point. The signs then move in a counterclockwise direction, ending with Pisces.

Exactly opposite the Ascendant is the Descendant, coinciding with the sign of Libra. If, as we have stated, the Ascendant is how we perceive ourselves, then the Descendant—exactly opposite—is how we perceive others, whether business associates or the public in general, but usually our romantic partners.

At right angles to the Ascendant and Descendant, at the upper part of the horoscope, coinciding with the sign of Capricorn, is the Midheaven, abbreviated as MC for the Latin phrase *medium coeli*, or 'middle sky." The

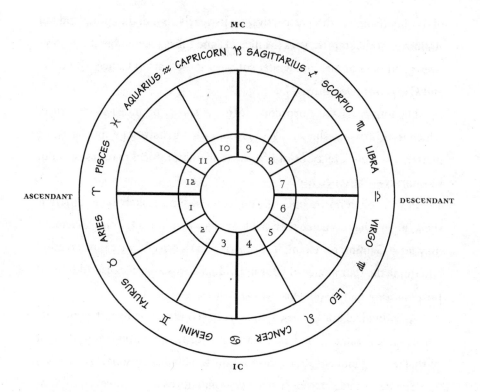

FIGURE 6

MC signifies how the world perceives you. It is how you "look" in society, whether through career, profession, any external status, or placement in life.

Exactly opposite the MC, at the base of the horoscope, coinciding with the sign of Cancer, is the *imum coeli*, or "inner sky," abbreviated as IC. If the MC is associated with public life, the IC signifies your private, or home life, representing your family as well as your memories and past.

The Ascendant, Descendant, MC, and IC are called the "angles" of the horoscope. They represent the four seasonal "turning points" of tropical astrology (from the Greek *tropikos*, meaning "to turn") that define the path of the Sun (from Earth's perspective) on its yearly round: the spring and fall equinoxes at the start of Aries (March 21) and Libra (September 22) respectively; and the summer and winter solstices at the start of Cancer (June 21) and Capricorn (December 21).

The angles of the horoscope form its spine, or internal structure, which in this case is shaped like a cross, called in astrology the "cross of matter," or four directions of life, symbolizing physical manifestation in its entirety—existence itself.

In your birth horoscope, the angles would most likely be in different signs (unless they coincide with the four signs mentioned). *Your* Ascendant may be in Gemini, for example, not Aries. In this book, we cannot readily determine the four angles of your individual horoscope because additional information of a personal nature is needed.

An individual horoscope requires special construction by rather intricate mathematical calculation based on your specific *date*, *time*, and *place* of birth. (See Appendix of Resources for how to obtain a personal horoscope.)

You do not need to construct a personal horoscope, however, to comprehend the basics of astrology. By examining the example horoscope, you can learn astrology's fundamental concepts. (Incidentally, today astrologers seem to favor the more colloquial term *chart* over horoscope. Accordingly, we will use these terms interchangeably. Also, a birth horoscope is commonly called a "natal" chart or horoscope.)

THE ECLIPTIC

Look at our example horoscope: The circle encompassing the twelve signs is nothing more than a rendition—in diagram form—of the Sun's path as it moves along the zodiac in the course of a year. The modern scientific term for this path is the *ecliptic*. The ecliptic is the yearly path of the Sun as seen from the perspective of Earth.

Along the ecliptic, as background, is the wide belt of star constellations, the zodiac, extending some eight degrees on either side of the ecliptic. As noted, the Greeks devised a system of dividing these constellations into equal thirty-degree segments—the pizza-pie slices—designating them as signs (and also houses).

All the planets, as seen from Earth, travel within this belt. In a completed horoscope they would all be placed in their respective signs. For our purposes, however, we will only place the Sun (in your particular Sun-sign) in it. Look at the example horoscope to perform this simple exercise:

> Place the glyph for the Sun, which is ☉, inside the pizza-pie slice that designates your particular Sun-sign.

If, for example, you were born between August 22 and September 22, you would place the glyph for the Sun in the segment designated by the word Virgo, as illustrated in Fig. 7.

THE HOUSES

Regardless of which sign you placed your Sun in, you will also note that your Sun will have an "address" for its location, a number from 1 to 12. This number represents the astrological house associated with your Sun-sign. If your Sun is in Aries, for example, it is also in the first house of the example horoscope; if in Taurus, it is in the second house, and so on.

In exploring the example horoscope further, you will notice that each of the twelve signs is marked off by a line that separates one sign (and house) from another. Each of these lines is known in astrology as a house

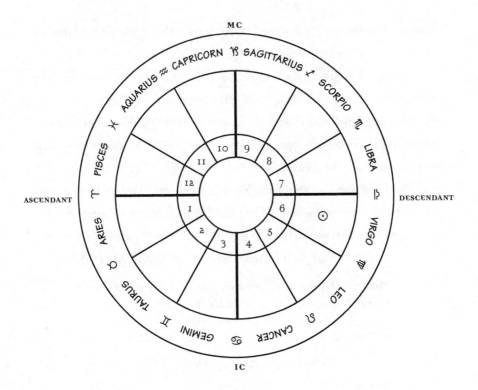

FIGURE 7

"cusp." In every chart, a house is always designated with a sign on its cusp, indicated with the glyph for the sign.

You will also notice that houses 1, 4, 7, and 10 coincide with the four angles of the horoscope. Accordingly, they are called "angular" houses. Houses 2, 5, 8, and 11 follow in succession and are called, aptly enough, "succedent" houses. The remaining houses, 3, 6, 9, and 12, are known as "cadent" houses. (The term derives from the Latin word *cadere*, which means "to fall." Cadent houses are said to "fall away" from the angles.)

As explained, a house signifies a special and particular arena of life. It is the place where a planet—the Sun in this case—operates, or "does its thing." In our exercise, for example, if you placed the Sun's glyph in the Virgo segment, your Sun is also in the sixth house of the horoscope.

The sixth house in astrology is, among other things, the house of your everyday job, work, and service. Your Sun in that house illuminates it; that is, it applies its solar strength and vitality to the affairs, interests, concerns, and activities of the sixth house's domain.

The Sun, the central body of our solar system, also symbolically stands for *your* own centrality. In its own special way, it serves as a kind of pronoun—as you do—as well as a verb in astrology; it is you with a capital *Y*. As a verb, it means "to express self-purpose and intention." In astrology, you enact or express your individual will, your sense of self—the very centrality of your being—by way of your Sun. The Sun's placement in a house is also where you "shine" in life, where you bring your unique illumination and light.

If your Sun is in the sixth house, therefore, we can construct a simple short story about you: "You place a great deal of your identity issues (Sun) onto your job—and work and service in general (sixth house). That is where you tend to shine and derive meaning and purpose to your life."

THE SIGNS

So far, in placing your Sun in the sixth house of the example horoscope, we have not described *how* you project, express, illuminate, or enact the Sun principles of self-identity in your work. Do you express your Sun's purpose at work by being assertive? Communicative? Sociable? Creative? How?

This is where the sign comes in. It describes the quality, style, or mode of operation that your Sun in the sixth house takes on to express your sense of purpose and self-identity on the job.

Using our example again, we see that the sign of Virgo stands for several qualities that surround work and service, including orderliness, exactness, and attention to detail. Therefore, in creating a simple, yet telling, beginning astrological story about you, we can also say that you place a great deal of your identity issues (Sun) onto your job, and work and service in general (sixth house), by performing tasks in a highly efficient, orderly, detailed—even perfectionistic—way (Virgo).

We have now combined the three main components of the horoscope—planet, sign, and house—to begin your story.

HOUSE SYSTEMS

In our example horoscope, each house cusp begins at zero degrees of each sign, with the signs and houses *exactly* coinciding. The Ascendant (the cusp of the first house) coincides with the start—at zero degrees—of the sign of Aries on March 21; the second house begins at zero degrees of Taurus on April 19, and so on. It is a horoscope based on what astrologers call an "equal house system," fashioned after the Greek scheme of twelve thirty-degree equal segments of the horoscopic circle.

This type of horoscope—with the start of Aries and the Ascendant exactly overlapping—is also known as the "natural astrological wheel," sometimes called the "flat wheel." It is the prototype for all horoscopes because it forms the basic structure of tropical astrology, which traces the Sun's path through the seasons of the year.

The natural astrological wheel, where the signs (starting with Aries) and houses overlap, is also the best and most simplified horoscope to use for understanding astrology because it shows, in diagram form, the natural affinity between each sign and its related house. In learning astrology it is essential to see the parallels between a sign and its corresponding house because they share symbolic meanings.

As illustrated in the natural astrological wheel—our example horoscope—every sign has a built-in connection with its related house. For example, the sign of Virgo has a correlation with the sixth house of work and service because Virgo is also oriented toward work and service in its quality of expression.

The Sun-sign of Virgo (you, "the Virgo," in popular parlance), therefore, encompasses in meaning both the sign of Virgo *and* the sixth house—as expressed by the Sun, which is also a kind of symbolic extension of you. Similarly, the Sun-sign of Scorpio, for example, encompasses in meaning both the sign of Scorpio and the eighth house, and so on.

When we separately describe each sign in the next chapter, we will also discuss the particular province of each house and how sign and house are connected.

Choosing a House System

There are many house systems in astrology, each dividing the horoscopic circle differently according to complex geometric formulas far too technical for the scope of this book. For constructing a personal horoscope, however, you must indicate to the chart service (see Appendix of Resources) which house system you want to employ. Today's two most frequently used house systems are the Placidus house system and the Koch house system.

Either one has equal value. (Your personal astrologer will have a particular preference among a variety of systems.)

No matter which house system you use, however, your angles (Ascendant, Descendant, MC, and IC) will be the same; only the intermediate house cusps (second and third; fifth and sixth; eighth and ninth; and eleventh and twelfth) will vary. Some astrologers cast charts in both the Placidus and Koch systems (or any number of other house systems) for comparative purposes.

THE RULING PLANETS

After stringing together our beginning astrological statement composed of planet, sign, and house—the Sun in Virgo in the sixth house in our example—we are ready to enlarge on your story by adding depth, breadth, and greater nuance of meaning. After all, you are much more complicated than a simple sentence!

In broadening your story, we must consider another factor in the horoscope in order to achieve a working knowledge of astrology's basic grammar. We have already pointed out that the Sun symbolizes a life principle that involves intent, purpose, will, identity—the very sense of self. But there are also other planets in the astrological firmament: Mercury, Venus, Mars, Jupiter, Saturn, Uranus, Neptune, Pluto, as well as the Moon. Each of these, in turn, symbolizes other life principles. (In Part III, we will discuss each planet and its special meanings in more detail.)

Mercury, for example, symbolizes the principle of service, among other things. (We will explore Mercury's several meanings in chapter 7.) The Roman god Mercury, known as Hermes to the Greeks, served the other deities by carrying messages for them; even today he is portrayed in some corporate logos as a fleet-footed messenger able to perform delivery services with speed and efficiency.

You may remember from chapter 2 that Mercury's predecessor was the Egyptian god Thoth, who also served as a kind of messenger or celestial aide, traveling back and forth from the Sun to the Moon and other planets. Other mythologies have deities embodying this type of activity because "to perform tasks or service" and, in a larger sense, "to connect two factors" is a universal principle of human behavior.

If we apply this concept to our example, just as the principle of service motivates the Virgo, and as service is the key activity of the sixth house arena of life, Mercury, in his service capacity, has a special affinity with Virgo and the sixth house. Stated astrologically, Mercury "rules" the sign of Virgo and the affairs of the sixth house. Mercury is the motivating factor behind that sign and house, calling the shots, as it were.

Although your Sun is in the sign of Virgo in the sixth house in our example, the real "owner" of the house is Mercury, not the Sun. The owner's sign, Virgo, is placed on the cusp of that house accordingly—just as any owner of a house would post a sign outside its door.

Thus, the planet Mercury, the sign of Virgo, and the sixth house form a kind of astrological triad, each in its own way sharing the same symbolic meanings. This is because Mercury is the ruling planet of the sign of Virgo and the sixth house.

But what about the Sun? If the Sun is in Virgo, as in our example, then both the Sun's symbolism *and* Mercury's symbolism become part of your story. The Sun is simply expressing itself in Mercury's house, "doing its thing" there—projecting self-identity in Virgo ways and in the arena of life that Virgo represents.

The Sun actually rules *another* sign and house—Leo and the affairs of the fifth house—not Virgo and the sixth house. The sign of Virgo and the sixth house derive their inherent meanings not from the Sun but from the symbolism around the planet Mercury.

Read this carefully, because to think astrologically takes a bit of practice!

The astrologer puts all these factors together (and more) to create your story by combining the various meanings and symbolisms to which we have just referred: planet (the Sun), sign (Virgo), house (sixth house), and ruling planet (Mercury). Aspects—touched on in chapter 2—add even more information as your greater story unfolds.

Bear in mind, however, that for the purpose of learning the basics of astrology, we are working solely with the natural astrological wheel—our example horoscope. In your personal horoscope, your Sun in Virgo may fall in a house other than the sixth house. (If you are a Gemini rising, for example, your Virgo Sun would likely fall in the fourth house of your natal chart. Since the sign of Virgo would now be on the cusp of the fourth house, Mercury would now rule the fourth house—but still be the "natural" ruler of the sixth house. Added also to the mix is the Moon, the "natural" ruler of the fourth house.)

To add even more to the complexity, the astrologer analyzing your natal chart also takes into consideration the house ruled by the Sun in your chart—in discussing your Sun in Virgo, for example. In the art of interpretation, *many* strands are woven together to form the unique and intricate tapestry that is *you*.

In Part III, we will discuss all the planets and the life principles they represent, as reflected in their Greco-Roman mythologies. However, in the next chapter's descriptions of signs, we will also explore each sign's ruling planet as it connects to their shared symbolism.

HOUSES, SIGNS, AND THEIR RULERS

1ST HOUSE:
Aries
ruled by Mars

2ND HOUSE:
Taurus
ruled by Venus

3RD HOUSE:
Gemini
ruled by Mercury

4TH HOUSE:
Cancer
ruled by the Moon

5TH HOUSE:
Leo
ruled by the Sun

6TH HOUSE:
Virgo
ruled by Mercury

7TH HOUSE:
Libra
ruled by Venus

8TH HOUSE:
Scorpio
ruled by Pluto; coruler, Mars

9TH HOUSE:
Sagittarius
ruled by Jupiter

10TH HOUSE:
Capricorn
ruled by Saturn

11TH HOUSE:
Aquarius
ruled by Uranus; coruler, Saturn

12TH HOUSE:
Pisces
ruled by Neptune; coruler, Jupiter

For now, let us simply return to our example horoscope, the natural astrological wheel. You have already placed your Sun in its corresponding sign and house. Now, by consulting the box above, put the name of the ruling planet (and, where pertinent, the coruler) for your Sun-sign below the word for the sign. (In our example, you would write Mercury below the word *Virgo*.)

Having done this, you now know not only your Sun-sign but also the house in which it falls in the natural wheel and the ruling planet for that house and sign. This forms your unique astrological profile that begins to tell your story in the simplest, yet fundamental terms.

SUMMARY

1. Your Sun in a sign tells you how you express your identity, purpose, and will.
2. The house it is in tells you where you focus a great deal of energy to accomplish this.
3. The ruler of the sign your Sun is in describes your psychological "motor," that is, the planet that drives the engine, which allows the Sun to accomplish its goals.

THE NATURAL ASTROLOGICAL WHEEL

By following the path of the Sun around the natural wheel —our example horoscope—you will meet up with your own Sun-sign along the way. In the process, you will come to understand how all the signs operate. You will also begin your acquaintance with your ruling planet (more about that planet, and its symbolism, in a later chapter). All of this, and more, can be grasped by way of the natural astrological wheel, with the Sun in Aries, the "first mover," setting the wheel in motion.

As the basis and rationale of tropical astrology, the natural astrological wheel underlies *all* personal horoscopes. For the practicing astrologer, progress in individual chart interpretation could not proceed properly without a core understanding of this wheel, because it serves as the original blueprint to which every astrologer implicitly refers when working on a natal chart.

Likewise, if you familiarize yourself from the start with the dynamics of the natural astrological wheel, you will be sufficiently able not only to fathom the inner meanings of your own Sun-sign but all other signs as well because you will have grasped astrological principles applicable to all horoscopes. And if and when you opt to obtain a personal horoscope, you will already know your ABCs, your *a*strological *b*asic *c*hart!

With this in mind, let us take a trip around astrology's natural wheel, moving as we go (counterclockwise) from sign to sign, from house to house, all the while tracing the Sun as it follows its yearlong path along the zodiac.

As we follow the Sun, we see how the signs reflect the myriad faces of nature as the seasons of the year unfold. We see too how human development also unfolds at different stages, or way stations, of life because the natural wheel serves as a kind of metaphor for the seasons of human life as well.

Such a trip, however, requires a special road map; we must know, literally, how to read the signs. A fuller rendering of the natural astrological wheel is called for, as illustrated in Fig. 8.

With this new diagram, we hope to capture for you a sense of the natural wheel—and by extension, your personal chart—as an entity that seems to vibrate, pulsating, as it were, in a kind of *yin-yang* pattern of active and receptive energies. In this way you can envision the horoscope as having a kind of heartbeat because it is dynamic, alive, and in the flow of life, just as you are.

Other than the *yin-yang* pattern, you will also notice in the diagram an alternating pattern of fire, earth, air, and water, each of which is connected to a particular sign. In astrology these four substances are called the

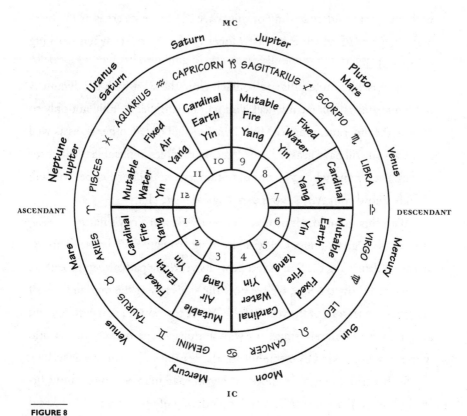

FIGURE 8

elements. They describe your basic chemistry, the "stuff" you are made of. If your Sun is in the sign of Aries, for example, your substance is said to be fiery; that is, you respond to life in a fiery—even tempestuous—way.

We will devote a later chapter to an in-depth exploration of the psychological implications of the elements in astrology. But for now, as we move through the seasons in the next chapter, you will see how the elements weave themselves into nature's fabric by way of the signs.

Signs in astrology are also said to be cardinal, fixed, or mutable, indicating with this a kind of behavior pattern, a modus operandi, if you will, that distinguishes a particular sign. These types of patterns are called, appropriately enough, the modalities in astrology, colloquially known as the "modes."

With road map in hand and the Sun as our guide, we can begin our trip around the wheel. Of course, as we progress you will want to see how your Sun, the very center of your being, resonates with the astrology of its sign.

The path of the sun:

Through the Wheel of Life

THE SIGNS OF THE ZODIAC

Before beginning any trip, it helps to know how many places you will visit—and how long you will stay at each one. On this particular journey, as we travel through each Sun-sign, we will stop at twelve different locales. The first stop will be Aries, the last one Pisces.

At each stop along the way, the Sun (your guide and alter ego) will take on the flavor of the place for the length of its stay in the sign—some thirty degrees of time, about a month. Of course, if you were born in that Sun-sign, you will feel immediately at home there, identifying with the character of the sign and its special features, which we will describe.

Using the latest version of our road map—the natural astrological wheel listing active and receptive principles, elements, and modes—we will explore the landscape of each sign, taking in its particular climate.

And, as we pass through each border—the cusp of each house—we will also come to know the ruler of the land, whose silent presence will be felt in the customs of its inhabitants. Later, you can read more about these influential rulers—in Part III of this book, which covers all the planets.

Bon voyage!

Aries

March 21–April 19

We begin our journey exactly at springtime—on the vernal equinox—at the sign of Aries. The Sun, heading north on its path, has just crossed the equator. Day and night are in momentary balance, but the Sun's light will now increase in the northern latitudes—and its fire will warm the wintered ground. It is a time of awakenings, buds, seedlings, shoots, and the sheer miracle of birth. Life is stirring in the earth again.

If you were born when the Sun was in Aries, you carry the imagery of spring within you; it is your psychic birthmark, an imprint of nature etched into memory. Aries—always the first sign of the zodiac on the natural wheel—is precisely about the initial, primal thrust that starts the wheel of life anew. In a similar way, your personality is imbued with drive, life force, spark, enthusiasm, a sense of action, of getting things going, of doing. Yours is a competitive, assertive sign, wanting to be first, to lead.

Aries energy is *yang*, penetrating, active. In its astrological modality, Aries is cardinal (the word *cardinal* literally means "first," "initiatory"). Cardinal also means red, the color of fire, which is your sign's astrological element. Your temperament is also fiery, passionate, dynamic, eager, and sanguine. You can also be hot-blooded, impetuous, reactive, impulsive, quick to anger, tempestuous, and feisty.

Since Mars, the Roman god of war, is your sign's ruler, you are highly capable of displaying heroic warrior qualities: bravery, daring; a kind of fearless ability to fight the good fight, to step into the fray, as well as rescue someone from danger; to aid.

In general, you like to win life's battles, but you are not out to destroy. You simply love to compete. You also love to take on a challenge—and, more rashly, a dare. If your natural assertiveness is negatively expressed, however, it can turn aggressive and combative, even reckless.

In the solar system, the planet Mars is the first planet "stepping out" into outer space away from Earth. This is a useful metaphor to describe your heroic impulse, which is a reflex to step forward, to face unknown perils, and to brave what lies ahead. Yours is the sign of the pioneer, the trailblazer, the person willing to break new ground, to venture unafraid into uncharted territory.

Aries is the sign on the cusp of the first house and the Ascendant in the natural wheel. Like the Ascendant, the first house in astrology is where you present yourself, where you put forth your personal style, your imprint. It is the house of the emerging ego, the newly manifested self, the person *as such* simply being in the world.

The first house is angular, which invests it with exceptional strength and power, since it sits on one of the four angles of the horoscope—in this case the Ascendant. (Accordingly, the fourth, seventh, and tenth houses are also angular.) The four angles of astrology are also called the cardinal points. Angular houses are associated with cardinal signs.

Psychologically, Arians seem to be invested with an abundance of libido, or life force. It is a kind of vitality that propels you into action, into exerting your personal will upon the world. There is also a kind of erotic charge to this type of energy because it stems from instinct, sexual drive, raw primal need, and impulse.

In life's developmental stages, Aries is the infant of the zodiac, bursting into life, proclaiming *me, I am*! And like the infant, Aries will kick and scream for what it wants, giving it the reputation of the "me-first" sign. Perhaps because of this, the Arian's unabashed affirmation of self is often mistaken for selfishness or unbridled egotism. This is not necessarily so, for me-first will also be first to jump from a bridge to save someone from drowning!

The word *Aries* stems from the Latin word for ram, the constellation associated with the sign. The ram is known to butt its horns—particularly against a rival—seeming to batter its way forward. The glyph for Aries, ♈, is literally a pictograph of horns.

In the physical body, Aries rules the head. The sign *is* about being headstrong, impatient, seeming to leap into things headfirst, head-on. Aries's rulership of the adrenals may also account for the sudden rush of blood to the head—that quick flash of anger so common to Arians.

Taurus
April 19–May 20

If the ram, Aries, is the irresistible force, then the bull, Taurus, is the immovable object. If you keep in mind the idea of the astrological wheel as a dynamic, pulsating entity, vibrating in a *yin-yang* pattern, you will see how each sign, in sequence, acts as a kind of counterbalance or corrective to the other.

So, if the *yang* force of Aries rushes headlong into things, then the *yin* force of Taurus receives, holds, stabilizes, and contains them. Likewise, where the cardinal modality of Aries initiates—but not necessarily sustains—then the fixed modality of Taurus seizes the thing, holds fast to it, and possesses and maintains it. And, by contrast, mutable Gemini, the next sign, flies from such fixed attachment.

When the Sun is in Taurus, the ground is ripening. It is rich, fecund, soft, already warmed by the Sun's rays. The birds, bees, and flowers thrive: Fertility abounds, and greenery is everywhere. The land smells of grass and meadow, animal, and loamy soil. The work of the plow—the bull's classic implement—has been done. The seeds have sprouted, the roots have been laid down; nature is pregnant with life.

If you were born when the Sun was in Taurus, these images of the fullness of nature comprise your inner vision; they make up your interior landscape, your psychic picture book. You also have a strong sense of it being your birthright to enjoy all this bounty, to partake of it wholly—for yours is a sensual, fertile sign, attuned to the comforts, pleasures, and richness of life. Indeed, the physical, material realm is your natural milieu.

However, appreciating the world's texture and beauty is only part of the picture. You also know that nature's rich produce is mostly yielded through effort, toil, and the sweat of one's brow. You know deep in your bones that everything of value has a price. Yours is an especially hardworking, steady, and productive sign, bent on extracting the goods of life you so ardently desire.

The sign of Taurus is often equated with the acquisition of money and wealth. This is because Taureans, in wanting the things that money can buy, are always working—to obtain more money! But if we think about it astrologically, for Taureans money simply represents the *physical* form of the sheer energy first initiated by Aries. Money is a tangible way to show the value of human effort. Taurus translates energy into a material form.

And, if we think about it psychologically, money for Taurus really represents security. Above all else, that is what you, the Taurean, seek and value most. Just as Aries is the sign of the pioneer, yours is the sign of the settler—preserving, cultivating, working, protecting, securing, and ultimately *owning* the land.

Your astrological element is earth, and your basic temperament is also earthy, grounded, practical, and sensible. Your personality is determined, stable, constant, solid. Yours is also an especially loyal and devoted sign. Your protective, preserving nature is "for keeps," but, if not controlled, it can also turn overly possessive and proprietary. If negatively expressed, your stolid determination and fixity can also turn into downright stubbornness, into a kind of bullheadedness.

Your real strength and power, however, like the bull's, are mostly held in reserve. And, like the bull, you are also placid, steady, enduring, and slow to anger. But when provoked—especially by the red flag of rage—you will charge with the fury of nature. When not directly challenged, however, a Taurean actually seems lazy, in a state of idle contentment. But do you remember the cartoon character Ferdinand the Bull? He always managed to be roused by the bee!

Taurus rules the neck, the throat, and the voice. The strength and flexibility of the bull are largely in its neck. In the bullfight, for example, the picador immobilizes the animal by lancing its neck muscles. And since Taurus also rules the weight-regulating thyroid gland, your sign seems to come in two distinct sizes: thick-necked and bulky or long and lanky.

The sign of Taurus is on the second house cusp of the natural astrological wheel. The second house concerns everything you hold in value:

money, possessions, resources, pleasures, property—or loved ones. It represents the things you want to keep. It is the house of your attachments. The second house (along with the fifth, eighth, and eleventh houses) is a succedent house. Succedent houses are associated with fixed signs.

As a developmental stage, Taurus is that time of life when the toddler clings to a toy, a biscuit—anything—while asserting the word *mine*. And in the same way that Aries actively proclaims *I am*, or *me*, Taurus will stolidly declare *I have*.

The glyph for the sign, ♉, depicts the head and horns of the bull, Taurus's constellation. In almost all cultures, the bull—as puller of the plow—is associated with fertility, wealth, and productivity, all of which are the sign's hallmarks. In our culture, for example, the bull stands as an emblem of financial progress, of "growing" wealth in an "up" market.

Since Venus, the goddess of love, is the ruler of Taurus, your sign is connected to the pleasure principle. You express love in a natural, physical, and sensual manner. The five senses—especially touch—appeal to you. The touch of Venus, in particular, inspires you greatly to be creative, productive, fertile, and prolific in all your efforts.

Gemini
♊
May 20–June 21

In keeping with the wheel's "vibration," when we come to the sign of Gemini, we meet up with everything that Taurus is not. Gemini's astrological mode is mutable—that is, changeable, variable, inconstant, shifting. Unlike Taurus's, yours is an energy that does *not* want to be contained, fixed in a secure place, or too greatly attached to a person, place, or thing.

Your astrological element is air. Your airy nature wants to fly, to leave the solid ground in which Taurus is so deeply rooted, and to head for the sky, away from the heavy bonds of fixed earth. You can see the flying Gemini spirit in such storybook characters as Peter Pan, the Little Prince, Tinker Bell, and in the flying carpet tales—or anywhere else where the mind is taken on flights of fancy.

At the time of Gemini, we are between the seasons. It is late spring; everything is in bloom, yet summer is not quite here. And, in keeping with our metaphor, the Taurean work of the fields is also done. Our mind is now free, and we are thinking of escape, of wandering off, of flight. We yearn to be carefree, light, free-spirited, to move on to other things: a trip to town or a neighboring community; perhaps to call on friends to chat or catch up on news.

If you were born when the Sun was in Gemini, you carry within you these kinds of stirrings; they are the moving clouds of your inner sky, your psychic firmament. You want your mind to be lifted up, like a cloud, and taken to different places because you feel the need to explore, to communicate, to exchange ideas.

You do not want to linger, however, because yours is a sign that needs variety, change, and constant stimulation. Your Gemini personality is restless, inquisitive, interested in ideas, and in all forms of mental activity, including words, language, speech, conversation, data, and information. If not adequately calmed, however, your energy can turn high-strung, fluctuating, and nervous—in a word, flighty.

Gemini is named for the twins, a constellation containing two great stars that seem to be locked in a perpetual embrace, each taking turns to brighten and darken. From this visual pattern, the idea is derived of your sign's "duality," of the two-sidedness that you so often express: You are characteristically noted for being "of two minds" about practically everything. It is hard for you to stay out, for example, because your twin is always calling you to come home! And, when you are home . . . well, you know the rest. Coming and going is your forte.

The glyph for Gemini, ♊, is the Roman numeral two. Reflecting its duality, Gemini is neither *yin* nor *yang*; it is both. Geminis, then, are often described as everything from ambidextrous to ambisexual. Yours is the most versatile—and curious—sign of the zodiac.

Gemini is the sign on the third house cusp of the natural astrological wheel. The third house is associated with siblings (the twins). It is the house of your immediate environment, representing your daily interactions and communications—not only with siblings but also with neighbors and casual acquaintances. The third house also represents short trips, especially for learning about things. It is a cadent house. (So are the sixth, ninth, and twelfth houses.) Cadent houses are associated with mutable signs.

Since Gemini's ruler is Mercury, the Roman messenger god, your sign is often described as mercurial—quick, able to jump from one thing to another. In mythology, Mercury was also associated with commerce, travel, and thievery. In this last sense, your Gemini spirit is often connected with cleverness, cunning, and even some deviousness.

There is a bit of the trickster in every Gemini. The clever little monkey of children's books, Curious George, perfectly exemplifies this mischievous, impish side of your sign. The monkey, like a Gemini, likes to flit (from tree to tree), from one thing to another, seeming to fly.

Mercury, with winged hat and feet, was envisioned as a flying god. Delivering messages, he flew from the heavenly heights down to the mortals below, constantly flitting between two worlds. On a symbolic level, he transmuted, that is, he could change from spirit (above) to matter (below) and back again. Like you, the communicative Gemini, he could weave and shift from one place to another, carrying an idea—something from on high—and putting it into material form (written language and speech).

In human development, Gemini represents that stage of life when the little child perennially asks "why?" It is a time of inquisitiveness, branching out to explore surroundings, and using language to communicate. The idea of two is also emphasized because the child is aware at this stage of being separate from its environment—hence, the need to investigate it and move around within it.

The physical dexterity of your sign is seen by its rulership of the hands, shoulders, and arms. Gemini also rules the two lungs, where carbon dioxide is exchanged for oxygen, as well as the nervous system, the busy switchboard that coordinates a wide variety of stimuli—like Gemini itself.

Cancer

June 21–July 22

At the time of Cancer, we are at a turning point on the seasonal wheel. This is the summer solstice, when the Sun seems to come to a standstill in the sky, giving us our longest day. It has reached its maximum elevation in the northern latitudes; it will soon pivot and begin its journey southward. The days will grow shorter, the nights longer.

The Mesopotamian astrologers called this turning point "the northern gate of the Sun," through which all souls descended as they came into physical being. They imagined this gate as the celestial womb of an incarnating world-mother from whom all life is spawned. The sign of Cancer, accordingly, signifies the mother in her fertile, nurturing aspect.

If you were born when the Sun was in Cancer, this life-giving, maternal imagery resonates within you; it forms your psychic matrix. Yours is a receptive, *yin* sign: containing, protecting, home-oriented, and personal. Your attitudes generally reflect a mothering, caring personality. Those you take into your life become instant family. Your devotion to them knows no bounds. If you carry this too far, however, your instinctive mothering can turn smothering.

The glyph for Cancer, ♋, resembles a kind of *yin-yang* configuration, which also stands for an eternal procreating force, an endless life-creating cycle. The glyph is also described by some astrological writers as breasts because your sign rules the breasts, as well as the womb and stomach.

Cancer's constellation is the crab, which the Greeks believed was placed in the sky by Hera, *their* great mother-goddess. Many crablike qualities belong to your sign: tenacity, indirect maneuvering, evasiveness, and a defensive shell that covers a soft, sensitive interior.

The crab also has a deep and mysterious connection to the moon tides, reflected astrologically by Cancer's rulership by the Moon. The Moon fluctuates, subtly shifting its shape as it waxes and wanes. Like you, it shows different "faces." There is no other sign in the zodiac whose emotions are as varied, nuanced, and wavering as yours. Cancer's connection with the Moon also imbues you with a reflective, soulful aura.

Your astrological element is water. Your temperament is similarly "watery," emotionally fluid. You are highly responsive, capable of great empathy for others. Your sensitivity, however, often makes you vulnerable to hurt, causing you to hide your feelings behind a self-protective demeanor of personal reserve.

Like Aries, Cancer is a cardinal sign, initiating a new season of the year. But Cancer is cardinal water, not fire. You tend, therefore, to tug or pull at your emotions, rather than push or assert what you want—as cardinal, fiery Aries might. Reflecting your sign's indirect, "crablike" qualities, you always make your desires known in a subtle and oblique way.

At the time of Cancer, we are actually in an inundation of water, with summer's rushing streams, flooded rivers, and water-laden fruit ripening on the trees. Mother Nature herself is as full as a womb. In human nature, Cancer represents the stage of life when the young child feels safe and contained within the bosom of home, family, and mother. It is a time when the sense of "belonging" is established, when the child knows it is part of an all-embracing unit, with common, familial roots.

Cancer's house on the natural astrological wheel is the fourth house, where a cardinal point, the IC (*imum coeli*, or inner heaven) is placed. The IC forms the foundation of our psychological being, incorporating such things as home, family, and our past with its store of personal memories. The IC is the root of our emotional history. It is also where, on a core level, we are "at home" with ourselves.

Correspondingly, the fourth house in astrology represents your literal home. It is the place of your domestic and family life. This includes your familial beginnings as well as where you presently live. The fourth house represents not only the idea of home itself but also all of its emotional connotations. It is the reservoir for our deepest and earliest feelings.

Home is also the place of return because we always return there at day's end. The fourth house, then, is a kind of personal, interior space—literally and figuratively—where you can close the door, kick off your shoes, and simply be yourself.

As the symbolic place of return, the fourth house is also the house of endings, as well as beginnings. Therefore, astrologers often refer to this house as both "womb" and "tomb," evoking with this your sign's ancient imagery as an eternal, procreating, generative force.

Leo
🦁
July 22–August 22

While the Moon-ruled sign of Cancer conjures up *yin* and watery qualities, the Sun-ruled sign of Leo expresses *yang* and fiery ones. Like the
Moon, Cancer is reflective, soft, and dreamlike in its nature. But you, the
Sun-ruled Leo, like to bask in the brilliance of your own light, radiating
fire and heat from your central core.

At the time of Leo, the Sun also beats down steadily on the land; it is
the very heart of summer. Nature's glories are on proud display. Our work
is done; it is time for play, pride in our accomplishments, and taking simple joy in life itself.

If you were born when the Sun was in Leo, *you* form the center of your
solar system because you carry an image within you of a glowing star,
ablaze in the middle of a psychic galaxy. And like the Sun itself, you exude
warmth, radiance, illumination, vitality, and power. By way of your sign's
rulership by the Sun, it is linked to consciousness itself, for the Sun is
emblematic of such things as visibility, clarity: seeing the light.

A fixed fire sign, your Leo energy burns with strength of purpose, con-
stancy, and sustained will—in contrast to the quick, initiatory spark of
Aries's cardinal fire. You are fiery, passionate, and aglow with an intensified, fixed energy. You also possess a kind of personal magnetism, or
charisma, that draws people in around you.

The word *Leo* is Latin for lion, your sign's constellation. Leo's glyph, ♌,
suggests the mane and tail of the lion. The bright triple-star Regulus (Latin
for king) sits at the heart of the lion constellation. The fabled king of the
beasts is traditionally connected with royalty, majesty, and power. This
capacity for leadership, for carrying the scepter of authority, is often found

in your sign. Leo also represents the individual's quest for *self*-authority, autonomy, and a sense of inner "kingship."

In the physical body, Leo rules the heart, back, and spine. To have backbone, spine, or heart is synonymous with having courage. Love also springs from the heart. Leo is full of heart and unafraid to love—as love is perhaps the greatest act of courage. The expression *lion hearted* (ascribed to King Richard I, who was brave enough to dethrone his powerful father) means "extracourageous."

Along with courage, you are also self-confident, loyal—and famously proud. Your pride, however, if carried to excess, can lead to the proverbial fall. And your confidence, if left unchecked, can turn to outright arrogance. But your primary Leo nature is sunny, fun-loving, playful, and even childlike. You will give of yourself with all your heart. Indeed, you can be generous to a fault.

Above all, yours is a dramatic, theatrical sign. As befits your nature, you prefer center stage, a starring role, and a round of applause as you enter the scene. Knowing this, it is fun to hear the magnificent lion purr. But get ready for an earsplitting roar if the hungry—for attention—creature is not given its due!

Leo is on the cusp of the fifth house of the natural astrological wheel. This is the house of "pride and joy," of children, and of childhood itself. In a related way, the fifth house signifies what you give birth to creatively. It represents your talents, capacity for self-expression, and dramatic flair, and the passionate involvement that *love* for something—or someone—brings.

Perhaps all of this explains why the fifth house is also called the house of risks (including gambling as well as "taking a chance on love"). It is the house of romance and the dating game, as well as fun, play, sports, and hobbies.

In human development, Leo depicts the stage of life where the child, venturing out from Cancer's protective world of home and family, steps onto the path of individuality and self-discovery. It is a time when the young child leaves the safety of the mother's realm for the riskier, more adventurous terrain of outside playmates, of other girls and boys.

Summoning courage, the youngster at this stage does battle in the outer world, heroically encountering the dramas of personal friendship—and the ardent crushes of young love. From this, the love affair with life really begins, for it is a time for the opening of the heart.

Virgo

August 22–September 22

The self-correcting, vibratory energy of the natural wheel is once again apparent in the contrast between your sign of Virgo and its Leo predecessor. For while Leo's *yang* energy is outgoing, self-celebratory, exuberant, and dramatic, your *yin* nature is private, reserved, modest, and unassuming.

And if Leo is the symbolic king, the royal majesty, then Virgo is the king's symbolic alter ego, the faithful servant. As such, service is the keynote word for Virgo; it is through service to others that you find yourself. Yours is a helpful, efficient, and productive sign.

At the time of Virgo, it is summer's end. Fall is just around the corner. The days are growing shorter, the weather cooler. In our metaphor, we now resume the labor of the fields. The crops, ripened under Leo's golden rays, must be picked, gathered, culled, sorted, bundled, and harvested; the fruit preserved, the corn stored, and the wheat, separated from the chaff, brought to mill. At summer's end, we return to the "daily grind," the routines and habits of regular life.

If you were born when the Sun was in Virgo, you inwardly follow the same theme of life's daily bread, of work, humble tasks, the service of your labor; it is your psychic almanac, the guide to your inner sky. The small, necessary details of everyday life give sustenance to your soul.

But as you consult your internal almanac, you know that the weather will change, because Virgo is a mutable sign. This imparts to Virgos a sense of nature's internal flux, of its organic, dissolving qualities—of how things eventually decay, breaking down to their smallest particles. Your personality, accordingly, is highly analytical; you are able to discern the infinitesimal yet ever-changing patterns in all of life.

Your element is earth, like Taurus's. You are earthy, practical, pragmatic, grounded, sensible. Like those born in Taurus, you concern yourself with physicality. But, while "fixed" Taurus seeks to keep things just as they are, mutable Virgo wants to examine life's inner workings, analyze its parts, and improve it—mostly by cleaning out its impurities and refining it. Virgos often focus on the physical body itself, as well as diet, health, hygiene, and nutrition.

The constellation associated with your sign is the virgin, depicted holding a sheaf of wheat. This suggests not only the productivity of your sign but also its symbolic connection to food. Virgo's astrological glyph, ♍, depicts the loop of the intestines, which it rules. The intestines are where we *do* really separate the wheat from the chaff—sorting what is useful from what should be discarded. Your pragmatic, discriminating, economical, and meticulous personality accords well with this metaphor.

Your sign's virgin motif imparts to you the attributes of modesty, scrupulousness, a high regard for the purity of the body, and a kind of moral spotlessness. However, these virtuous qualities can also often be your means of avoiding intimacy, of remaining emotionally intact, unpenetrated. Yours is an exacting sign. In noticing flaws in others, you often try to make them over because, above all else, you seek perfection. Not finding it, you may shun closeness entirely.

But you reserve your severest criticism for yourself. Self-improvement is the hallmark of your sign and self-perfection its ultimate goal. Failing to achieve these, the Virgo sometimes gives up completely. When this happens, we meet up with what astrologers call the "sloppy Virgo," whose house is in disorder, dishes piled in the sink, papers in disarray, clothes strewn across the floor—all in all, a *perfect* mess!

Your sign's ruler, Mercury, in his flying messenger guise, traveled through the air like a Gemini, transmuting from spirit to matter. With earthy Virgo, however, Mercury's transmuting process takes place in the physical body. With digestion, food (matter) is turned into energy (spirit). In a kind of parallelism, words (Gemini's realm) are often linked with the assimilation of food (Virgo's realm). We absorb, digest, and chew on food and ideas. We see this connection in such expressions as "food for thought," to "digest" or "absorb" an idea, to "eat" one's words, and so on.

Virgo is on the cusp of the sixth house of the natural astrological wheel. In accord with your sign's signature, this is the house of your workaday world—its duties, tasks, and services. It represents such things as your job, coworkers, employees, and labor in general. The sixth house is also associated with your physical health, the care of your body, and your daily habits and routines.

Developmentally, Virgo represents the stage of life when the young person learns the importance of practical wisdom and sensibly adapting to the rules and habits of an ordered life. It is a time for schooling and preparing the ground for the social and intellectual tasks that lie ahead. It is the time of life when the youngster takes up a craft, hobby, service, or job.

We see your sign at work in organizations like the Girl Scouts, the Boy Scouts, the 4-H clubs, as well as in recycling, ecology, and health and fitness programs. In a corresponding way, you express the qualities of your sign by being of service to others, honing your skills, and improving and refining yourself. Because you know that God is in the details, by perfecting yourself, you are also perfecting the world.

Libra
♎
September 22–October 23

In the sign of Virgo, we have completed the process of tracing the developing self within the six arenas of life that encompass the formative years of childhood. In a similar sense, the bottom half of the wheel is considered to be the sphere of the inner, subjective, personal realm.

When we step into Libra's seventh house, we cross a threshold into the outer, objective, social realm of life. In crossing this threshold—the cardinal point called the Descendant—we begin a kind of balancing process in which we proceed to integrate the "otherness" of the outer world. In this process, the outer world becomes, by turns, both a reflection and a projection of the developing self.

The initial balancing begins, aptly enough, with the scales—Libra's constellation. As we step onto the scales of Libra, it is the first time on our journey around the wheel that we can "look across" at a sign we have already visited, namely the opposite sign of Aries.

In astrology, a sign together with its opposite sign is called a "polarity." A polarity encompasses symbolic counterparts. In the Aries-Libra polarity, Libra is the "thou" to Aries's "I."

In your sign of Libra, for example, you first recognize the separate other (symbolically, Aries), who is experienced as a kind of reflection of yourself. As you encounter the other, you psychologically are able to "see" yourself in relation to that other. Yours is the sign that symbolizes relatedness itself. Marriage, partnership, or any other form of serious, committed relationship is of paramount importance to you.

The glyph for Libra, ♎, depicts the Sun over the horizon, indicating the balance of night and day. At the time of Libra, we are at the autumn equinox, in exact seasonal opposite to the spring equinox. The Sun, heading south since its turn at the summer solstice, has again crossed the equator.

The Sun's light is decreasing in the northern climes, and its coddling warmth is slowly being withdrawn. As nature's seasonal clock ticks, night and cold will soon prevail. But for now, a balance is struck between summer's heat and winter's frost.

In our metaphor, at the time of Libra, the harvest is complete; everything has been gathered. Crops not stored for personal use are brought to the marketplace. There, the produce is bartered, bought and sold, balanced on the scales, and weighed and measured. It is a time of human interaction, sociability, exchange, and connectedness—a time too for courtship and finding a mate, since the long winter months lie ahead.

If you were born when the Sun was in Libra, this is the imagery you mirror within; it is your psychic ballast, your balancing rod. You thrive on the equal give-and-take of human affairs and on finding the proper, appropriate measure in your dealings with others.

Yours is the sign of the handshake, the reciprocal nod, the mutual smile, the tactful exchange of words. Your astrological modality is cardinal, and you seek to initiate social activities, partnerships, and alliances—all for the purpose of unity, merging, and relating. Above all, you seek a harmonious balance with others. The idea of balance is further amplified by Libra's ruling of the kidneys, the organ that regulates the body's balance of water.

Your sign's ruler, Venus, as expressed before through earthy Taurus, embodied love as a physical, natural pleasure, an experience of the senses. With airy Libra, however, Venus's symbolic process takes place in the abstract realm. You view love as an ideal, a romantic concept—one that is not especially rooted in bodily expression. Simply, you are in love with love. You believe in love's storybook version, refined and courtly, enacted as a kind of formal mating dance of bows and curtsies, replete with hearts and flowers. For those born in your sign, therefore, love is a form of aesthetics, more pleasing than pleasurable. It is Venus perceived as beauty, harmony, proportion, grace, and balance.

Like airy Gemini, airy Libra is a mental sign. But, while Gemini stands for the left-brain, literary, intellectual mind, Libra expresses right-brain imagery: art, form, elegance, the kind of sensibility we associate with good taste. The idea of fairness is deeply inherent too in Libra's nature. Fairness means beauty and justice alike—perfectly exemplified by the famous statue of blindfolded Venus, the symbol of beauty, holding the scales of justice. (Interestingly, Venus holds a sword, which is the symbol for Aries, in her other hand.)

Your fair-minded, just, Libran personality reflects your innate willingness to cooperate and share. You are accommodating, thoughtful, and diplomatic. But in your quest for fairness and making the right choice, you are also known to be indecisive and to equivocate.

Also, in your desire to accommodate others, you may often lose sight of your own preferences and needs. As a result, the scales inevitably start to tip too favorably toward the other person, and eventually fall out of balance.

When that happens, the fairy-tale romance does not have a happy ending—Prince Charming turns into a frog, and Beauty turns into the Beast!

Libra's seventh house is the house of relationship, signifying your partner as well as issues concerning partnership itself. It is also the house where you often project unfulfilled Aries-like strivings onto your significant other rather than live them out for yourself. On the developmental level, Libra represents that time of life when the individual marries, establishes a live-in or serious relationship, or a business partnership.

Although Libra is *yang* in its energy, it also stands for a kind of inner marriage, a symbolic union of opposites. It encompasses, psychologically, both *yin* and *yang*, as part of the sign's profound relatedness. Perhaps this is why some kind of role reversal invariably occurs with Librans, enabling them to put themselves in another's shoes—sometimes quite literally, with subtle gender-bending. Generally, however, the "switch" simply takes the form of assuming a nontraditional role in a relationship.

Scorpio
♏
October 23–November 22

In Libra, the horoscope maintains for the moment its equilibrium, poise, and grace. However, the astrological wheel keeps turning; it cannot remain still for long. After Libra, we come to the sign of Scorpio, where we recognize that even the loveliest of objects casts a shadow. In Scorpio, we deepen, intensify, and darken the soft, pleasing, pastel shades of Libra's refined palette.

Because where there is love—with all its niceties—there are also the nasties, ready to spring, as if from Medusa's head: jealousies, rages, compulsions, coercions, unbridled passions, obsessions—love's multitude of sins. And where there is diplomacy—with all its genteel mannerisms—there is also the hidden struggle for power, the practice of secrecy, and the unspoken wish to control another's resources. With Scorpio, we are compelled to acknowledge that Beauty and the Beast can, indeed, inhabit the same psyche.

Scorpio's ruler, Pluto, was the Roman god of the dead, reigning over the shadowy, mysterious realm beneath the earth. In a corresponding way, Scorpios project an air of mystery; they seem to be imbued with a kind of deep, even dark, secret power.

Before the planet Pluto was discovered, Mars was the ruler of Scorpio and today remains a coruler. As a Scorpio, you experience and express Mars's warrior nature, but in a more intense, longer, and drastic way than an Arian does. Yours is a fixed sign; you do not forget a slight easily.

Like Cancer, Scorpio is a *yin*, water sign. But, while the Moon's pull makes Cancers moody, their emotions seeming to ride the high and low tides of the sea, your fixed, intense emotions do not waver. Their watery sources seem to originate in impervious underground springs, deeply embedded beneath the surface. This explains your incredible capacity for emotional depth, intimacy, and passion.

At the time of Scorpio, dying autumn leaves have fallen to the ground. But the leaves are fodder for the soil, enriching the earth as they decay. This process gives promise to a kind of rebirth, a regeneration of physical matter after its transformation. Death is a part of a natural cycle, as it ultimately renews all life.

If you were born when the Sun was in Scorpio, life's unending cycles form your psychic pathway through the dark; they are recesses etched into your soul. You have the capacity to regenerate, to "die a thousand deaths"—

only to reinvent yourself a thousand times. You are resourceful, able to extract power, strength, and almost supernatural energy from seemingly hopeless, even impoverished, "dead" conditions.

In a parallel sense, this is reflected in your sign's ruler, Pluto. In mythology, Pluto was also known as the lord of hidden wealth. If we think about this, we see that so much of the world's resources are actually extracted from beneath the ground—Pluto's realm of the dead. These include all the fossil fuels; and iron ore, gold, silver, and other precious metals; diamonds, resins, and minerals; and the underground springs themselves, which feed the earth, as well as rivers, streams, and lakes.

Scorpio's constellation, the scorpion, is a solitary creature whose image conjures up mystery—and danger. The raised arrow of Scorpio's glyph, ♏, represents the scorpion's erectile tail, poised to deliver the sting of its deadly venom.

The raised arrow is also a symbol for sexual libido, suggesting a connection between sex and death. The French actually speak of sexual orgasm as a "little death." And some psychologists attribute postcoital *tristesse*, a deep sadness often occurring after orgasm, to a kind of near-death experience. Since Scorpio also rules the body's sexual organs—vital for procreation—we can see how sexuality, death, and regeneration are intertwined in your sign's constellation of energies.

Scorpio is also associated with three levels of manifestation, symbolized by the scorpion, eagle, and phoenix—the last, a mythological bird that rose from the ashes of destruction. This triad illustrates your sign's great emotional range. For while the lowly scorpion clings to the shadows, the mighty eagle soars toward the Sun. You the Scorpio are similarly capable of both scaling the heights of emotional experience and penetrating its depths, always—like the phoenix—renewing yourself in the process.

The polarity of Taurus and Scorpio represents the principle of desire. But while Taurus stands for personal desire—the simple satisfaction of the physical senses—Scorpio signifies shared desire, the *eros* principle so vital for creating new life. Developmentally, Scorpio is a time when the person deepens his or her emotional life, intimacy, and sexuality.

Scorpio is the sign on the cusp of the eighth house of the natural astrological wheel. This is the house of inevitabilities, like death and taxes, as well as compulsions, obsessions, secrets, and sex. It is also the house whereby you partake of other people's resources—by way of inheritances, wills, trusts, estates, legacies, and insurance—plus any other riches extracted from the dead!

Sagittarius

November 22–December 21

When we reach the sign of Sagittarius, the Scorpio emotions are channeled. They are converted and released into external, socialized passion. This process is depicted in a symbolic way through Sagittarius's constellation, the centaur: half horse, half human. The human half, poised with bow and arrow on a distant goal, rises above its animal body as if to supersede it. This suggests a moving away from the instinctual, or purely animal level, to human consciousness.

The figure is also known as the archer, its arrow imagery similarly evoking human aspiration, the striving for something beyond oneself. The glyph for Sagittarius, ✗, is also plainly an arrow, again reinforcing the goal-oriented, archer motif. The arrow also depicts the straightforward, active, direct, *yang* nature of the sign.

At the time of Sagittarius, fall is ending. The days are growing short and gloomy, the nights are too long. As if to dispel the dark, a kind of wanderlust and desire for change set in. We long to explore, expand, stretch our legs, have an adventure or two, head for sunshine. We also seek the light of knowledge, feeling the need to study, learn, and broaden our world, as we seek to find our place in the larger scheme of things.

If you were born when the Sun was in Sagittarius, you carry this boundless universe within you; it is your psychic macrocosm, your expanding world. Your guiding principle is growth, development, the search for wisdom and understanding, and the broadest scope of comprehension. You are the quester of the zodiac, seeking the Holy Grail—something that will add meaning to your life.

Your astrological element is fire. You are fiery, inspired, expressive, and aspiring; you are full of enthusiasm for projects and the possibilities of things. Your personality is exuberant and full of hope and optimism. You are jovial, good-humored, and positive. Yours is the sign of "yes, I can!"

But Sagittarius is also a mutable sign. Your passion often dissipates the closer you get to your goal. You are restless in your questing, constantly seeking change—whether of venue, a new outlook, or a fresh sense of purpose. There is a sense that you not so much need to find your goal as search for it; that you not so much have to arrive somewhere as experience the trip itself.

There is a bit of Dorothy of *The Wizard of Oz* in every Sagittarian's soul, always reaching for the elusive Emerald City in the faraway distance—somewhere over the rainbow. And even back in plain old Kansas, the Sagittarian happily proclaims, "Who cares if it was only an illusion? Just look at the wonderful people I met along the way!"

Gemini and Sagittarius form a polarity. Each wishes to fly, not to linger. Gemini (adjacent to Taurus) flies to escape the ground. Sagittarius (adjacent to Scorpio) flies from emotional depth, often causing Sagittarians to stray or simply wander away from commitment.

Sagittarius rules the hips and thighs. Although Sagittarians are noted for being physically sturdy, they also seem to struggle with weight, often indulging themselves too much. The sign also rules the liver, the organ that not only processes food and drink but is also highly sensitive to an excessive intake of both.

Since Jupiter, the Roman god of law and justice, rules your sign, you may also concern yourself with the civic side of life by taking up causes. Your aim is to improve society's lot. If necessary, you would teach, preach, moralize, philosophize, guide, and counsel to accomplish this. But you also travel, learn, and study whenever and wherever you can—for self-improvement as well as for a societal purpose.

Sagittarius is on the cusp of the ninth house of the natural astrological wheel. This is the house of travel and adventure, where we globe-trot, backpack, or simply roam the earth. Your house signifies your search for a larger truth, an "answer" to life—whether in the university, church, ashram, temple, or on your individual quest. In a related way, the ninth house is also connected with such things as law, ethics, philosophy, publishing, and higher education.

Developmentally, at the stage of life represented by Sagittarius, the individual explores other cultures, pursues advanced studies, and also seeks some sort of mentor or guide. It is also a time for developing a comprehensive philosophy of life, a belief system, or worldview because the individual aspires to formulate the moral, ethical, and religious principles necessary for the structure-building phase of the next sign, Capricorn.

Capricorn

The sign of Capricorn is named for the goat constellation, sometimes called the sea goat. The imagery of the goat, a mountain-climbing animal, is rather apt for our own journey around the astrological wheel because we have now climbed to the top of *our* mountain. We are at the MC (*medium coeli,* or Midheaven), the most elevated position of the horoscope.

The MC, like the Ascendant, IC, and Descendant, is a cardinal point, comprising the fourth and final angle of the horoscope's structural cross. As we stated earlier, the MC signifies how the world perceives you—it indicates your outer status in society. This usually manifests itself in such areas as your career, profession, title, and reputation.

The "climb" to reach the MC's high placement belongs to your Sun-sign, Capricorn. You are ambitious and seek success, which also means that you are disciplined, serious, and responsible in everything you set out to do. Yours is a cardinal sign, as you are driven to achieve high marks in your chosen field. You will not hesitate to initiate any required projects to meet your goals.

Equally, the tenth house, where the MC is, represents the arena of life that encompasses these concerns. The sign of Capricorn is on the cusp of the tenth house on the natural wheel. Accordingly, it is the house of your worldly occupations, the place where you live out your outer authority. In real terms it signifies your actual profession or career, and the struggles, successes, and failures that go with it.

As a developmental stage, Capricorn stands for that time of life when the individual views career as a serious matter and focuses on establishing a profession. No longer content with Sagittarian "searching," the individual devotes time and energy to "finding." The knapsack is now traded in for the briefcase.

At the time of Capricorn, the seasonal wheel has turned again, and we are now at the winter solstice. The Sun, seeming for the moment to stand perfectly still in the sky, pivots, returning north to us. The days grow longer, the nights shorter. This is the nativity of the Sun, ushering in the resurrection of light.

Still, the ice remains until the thaw. Frost covers the trees, the air is cold, the earth is still hard and unyielding. The landscape is somber, gray, bleak. Life feels solitary, melancholy because there is much darkness to get through before we can see the light. It is a time to make do with available resources.

If you were born when the Sun was in Capricorn, this is the cold night sky you carry within; it is your psychic reality. You are austere, conservative, pragmatic, and economical—but also patient, as you have a sense of life's eventual rewards, of light at the end of the tunnel, literally.

Like the goat climbing the mountain, you are also methodical, steady in your purpose, yet cautious and prudent. And just as the goat must grapple with the physical terrain, you, the Capricorn, are also always struggling with reality and its demands. Your astrological element is earth, but it is rocky; the ground is shaky and uphill.

Perhaps this is why Capricorn is often described in astrology as an insecure sign. Capricorns typically experience uncertainty underfoot—a feeling of limitation, one they believe they must always live with. In keeping with the horoscope's internal vibration, however, Capricorn's restrictive nature is a kind of corrective to its expansive predecessor, Sagittarius.

However, it is this very insecurity that often propels Capricorns, because they compensate by trying harder, by overcoming their obstacles.

Capricorns persevere, steadily pushing themselves onward and upward. It is the sign of self-mastery, self-control, the will to accomplish. It is also the sign of the classic workaholic, the type A personality, and the overachiever.

Your sign rules the knees, which are so vital for climbing. It also rules the bones and the skeletal structure in general, as well as the teeth, which are hard and bonelike, and the nails. The various processes of hardening (calcifying, consolidating, contracting, and crystallizing) all belong to Capricorn.

Yours is a *yin* sign, forming a polarity with Cancer. Capricorns, like Cancers, cover their sensitivity—and insecurity—with a self-protective shell of reserve. The glyph for Capricorn, ♑, depicts the sea goat, its horns at the upper segment, a fish's tail at the lower. The fish, with its watery motif, also suggests Capricorn's sensitive, emotional underpinnings.

Saturn, Capricorn's ruler, was the Roman god of agriculture. In agriculture, there is also a need to consolidate resources, plan ahead, and organize time. In the same way, Capricorns have a deep respect for the strict laws of nature and their relation to the passage of time. "To every thing there is a season, and a time to every purpose under the heaven." Capricorn's often somber cast may stem from a profound understanding of the internal workings of the cosmic clock as it ticks off the seasons of our lives.

Aquarius
♒
January 19–February 18

As we get to the sign of Aquarius, we still retain Capricorn's imagery of climbing the mountain. Because if we were preoccupied in Capricorn with the hardships of the climb itself, in Aquarius we are finally breathing in the purified, heady air at the top. There, we can also now see the wide panorama of small cities and villages below and experience a sense of an abstract humanity stretching over a vast, yet common territory.

Aquarius, an air sign, represents the mind at its most objective, detached, and impersonal level. You the Aquarian have the capacity to see the larger picture, and from this to envision abstract, universal truths. Your sign is also fixed in its modality, which means you hold fast to your lofty ideals and high principles.

You also translate these ideas into action because your sign is *yang*. There is nothing of the armchair philosopher about you. You join groups and forge friendships with like-minded people based on your interests and concerns, wanting to share what you know. As an Aquarian, you have "been to the mountain" and are poised to bring back your knowledge to the people below in order to make a better world.

One of your most cherished ideals is that of the human race as a single, unified entity, with shared values of common good. Yours is a one-world type of outlook. Another one of your most cherished ideals is that of the single, unique individual, endowed with the inalienable right to personal freedom, nonconformity, and independence. This is an anti-group outlook.

If these two concepts seem contradictory yet oddly compatible, you have captured the essence of your rather unusual Aquarian nature. You are quirky, idiosyncratic, eccentric, and original in your thinking. You have the uncanny ability to hold opposing views and keep them intact—yet somehow transcend them.

At the time of Aquarius, we are in the very heart of winter. Ice, wind, sleet, and snow abound. But as we look out on the landscape, we can see the approaching light as a new dawn awakens. However, the Aquarian month also represents the winter of our lives; we have planted our seeds, watched them grow, and reaped our harvest. What single truth can we now impart to others? It is this above all: Each strand of the human tapestry fits into the grand design.

If you were born when the Sun was in Aquarius, this is your psychic vista, your overview of life; it forms the pattern of your mind's eye. You are able to weave your singular life into the fabric of all life. You can see the interrelatedness of all things.

Aquarius forms a polarity with the sign of Leo. While Leo, the symbolic king, embodies a kind of royal prerogative, Aquarius symbolically represents the aristocracy of the people and, by extension, the nobility of the person, the single individual. In similar fashion, you, the Aquarian, pay little heed to distinctions of class, color, religion, ethnicity, gender, or any of the other artificial boundaries that separate people.

Yours is the most unconventional, freethinking, and open-minded of all the signs in the zodiac. But there is also a kind of paradox here—as in everything about your sign. While Aquarians encompass a vision of a common, unified world, their nonconforming attitudes often put them at odds with a majority of the people in it. In a related way, your sign is associated with such figures as the maverick, the inventor, the genius, the rebel, and the revolutionary.

In another variation of your sign's paradoxical nature, Aquarians, while holding humanity in high regard, often lack the capacity for true one-on-one intimacy. They are essentially detached, which often makes it difficult for them to connect emotionally to others. They tend to shy away from the messy, waterlogged affairs of personal matters.

Uranus, Aquarius's ruler, was the earliest sky-god of the Greco-Roman pantheon and was portrayed in myth as a distant figure. Before the planet Uranus was discovered, Saturn was the ruler of Aquarius, and today remains a coruler. The agriculture god's influence still permeates the sign, because Aquarians are innately aware of the step-by-step progress and arduous effort they must make in order to achieve their high ideals. They work tirelessly, especially in groups, to accomplish this.

Aquarius is on the cusp of the eleventh house of the natural astrological wheel. This is the house of group objectives, networking, and friends who share common values and goals. Many astrologers call it the house of hopes, wishes, and dreams because the eleventh house encompasses your highest aspirations—not only for yourself but also for the world at large.

We see the Aquarian signature in such places as the United Nations (especially its humanitarian agencies), international relief organizations, and space-exploration programs, which imply our commonality as Earth people.

In the physical body, Aquarius rules blood circulation, which also illustrates the idea of a single, unifying system for the whole organism. The sign also rules the shin and ankles, which link the knees (ruled by Capricorn) to the feet (ruled by Pisces), matching the zodiacal order.

Developmentally, Aquarius signifies the stage of life when the individual wants to give back to society what has been gained from the climb to the top in Capricorn. This is also symbolized by Aquarius's constellation, the Water Bearer, which depicts a kneeling figure pouring forth waters into the open celestial space below it.

What emanates from the vessel is not ordinary water, however, but a kind of vitalizing energy force. The glyph for the sign, ♒, also suggests electrical energy waves. These paradoxical images are somehow apt for Aquarius. The sudden flash of genius is a typical Aquarian vibration, as is the electrifying idea.

Pisces

February 18–March 20

Last but not least, we come to the sign of Pisces, a yin, mutable, water sign. In Pisces, we leave the cool, mountainous heights of Aquarius's intellect for the warm, curative waters of feeling and emotional depth. And, if in Aquarius our vision was looking outward, fixed from above on human consciousness, in Pisces we turn our vision inward, imagining a place of God-consciousness in the human world.

For you, the Piscean, that inward-looking place is mysterious and indescribable yet very real. It is a place where you dream, have visions, hear voices, imagine, and yearn. It is also where you experience spiritual longing, or what we might call "soul-connection," a relationship with something deeply indwelling yet inexpressible—except perhaps through art, music, dance, or poetry.

At the time of Pisces, the seasonal year is winding down, but night is still longer than day. We await the arrival of spring, when the Sun's light will finally prevail, as we emerge from the darkness of winter. The ice is dissolving, the howling winds subsiding, and the snows melting.

We have also lived through the seasons of life. World-weary by now, we accept the ending of our particular journey, secure in the belief that what ends is also a beginning—because the wheel of life will continue to roll along, each spoke of the wheel propelling the next.

If you were born when the Sun was in Pisces, you abide by this article of faith; it is the psychic covenant within your sacred sanctuary, your inner shrine. Sacrifice, letting go, dissolving—a kind of yielding up the ego-self— are some of your sign's keynotes.

Yours is the sign of spirituality or, more precisely, of spiritual love. The Greeks called this type of love *agape,* distinguishing it from *eros* (erotic desire), and from *amor* (personal or romantic love). In the early Christian church, agape was also a special "love feast" that accompanied the bread and wine of Holy Communion.

In your own Piscean manner, you long to bring this spiritual type of love into the world. You express this through acts of kindness, compassion, mercy, and sympathy, which are truly your outstanding traits. But these very traits can also translate into victimhood, the bane of your sign, for you tend to overidentify with others, losing yourself in the process. And by relinquishing your own needs, wants, and requirements, you often end up feeling sorry for your (lost) self.

Pisces comes from the Latin word for fish, your sign's constellation. Actually, they are two fish—swimming in opposite directions, one northerly, one southerly—their tails conjoined by a single star. This star was imagined by the ancients as a rope, or yoke, that ties the two fish together.

The image of the yoked yet separating fish is rendered pictorially in Pisces's astrological glyph, ♓. The yoked fish also evoke Pisces's innate duality—along with the sign's self-negating nature. As one side is pulled down into the dreamy, uncharted depths of the psychic sea, the other side is equally pulled up into the stream of life.

Similarly, Pisceans are often noted for elusiveness, uncertainty, and confusion. They long to escape life's involvements, often renouncing the ways of the world as sheer illusion. Still, they are constantly drawn back into reality, pulled by those irresistible "ties that bind."

Pisces rules the feet. To be barefoot is a kind of emblem for unattachment to worldly pursuits and of humility. But the feet are also those parts of the physical body that make contact with the ground, signifying a kind of connectedness to earthly pursuits. This ambiguity of meaning again reflects Piscean duality—both the sign's worldliness and its other-worldliness.

Neptune, Pisces's ruler, was the Roman god of the sea. Like the sea, Pisceans are uncontained by boundary, as they feel enveloped, and often submerged, by a kind of emotional vastness that can overwhelm them. They periodically seek refuge in islands of solitude, removing themselves entirely from people, places, and things. Although Pisceans have a strong psychological need to plumb their inner depths, they can sometimes also sink into them. Piscean means of escape, therefore, range from artistry to alcoholism.

Before the discovery of the planet Neptune, the ruler of Pisces was Jupiter, who today remains the sign's coruler. The influence of the god of law and justice is felt in the Piscean soul as karma, the Hindu and Buddhist principle of spiritual reckoning and a form of divine justice that takes its effect through successive lifetimes.

Pisces is the sign on the cusp of the twelfth house of the natural wheel. The twelfth house is described in astrology as "behind the scenes"—a place that is hidden, secret, or simply invisible to others. It represents such sites as asylums, hospitals, cloisters, retreats, or anywhere that we go for solace, healing, privacy, and inner peace.

The twelfth house is also the place we escape to for secret trysts, assignations, and love affairs—since Pisces, the sign of illusion, is also the sign of deception!

Virgo and Pisces form a polarity. Each of these signs devotes itself to service. But, while Virgo wants to find, or define, itself through service, Pisces seeks to *lose* itself through service. Developmentally, then, Pisces is a time for charity, volunteer work, or any other type of selfless service to others.

Pisces also signifies a time when the individual seeks to connect to psychic life through such activities as art, music, poetry, occult studies, meditation, or depth psychology. At this late stage of life, the individual desires at last to fulfill those treasured dreams, visions, and yearnings that were secretly tucked away during a lifetime of climbing the mountain.

With the last sign of Pisces, then, we complete our journey around the wheel, immersed, for the moment, in the purifying, baptismal waters of your sign's spiritual depths. But as the wheel turns, we ready again for that other baptism—the one by fire—as we spring anew into life, in the sign of Aries, proclaiming for all the world to hear: "I am!"

chemistry class:

The Four Elements of Astrology

THE INVISIBLE WORLD Of HUMAN CHEMISTRY

What is that magical thing called "chemistry," which draws two people together? Or the lack of which leaves two others cold? We often look at people who are good friends, enduring lovers, successful business partners, or strong mates and wonder what special glue could hold them together. How does it work? What are its ingredients? And where can we get some?

Obviously, the reasons people stay together are complex and do not lend themselves to a single answer. But that elusive thing called chemistry is undoubtedly one of them—and a powerful one. We are not talking about just physical chemistry, although that may be a crucial factor for some. There is also mental chemistry, a meeting of the minds, and emotional chemistry, shared feelings and values. We light each other's fire in more ways than one.

Paradoxically, what one person "sees" in another is largely invisible, like the molecular world of chemistry itself. We would need a special microscope to find out how their separate natures mix, how they cohere with—or even repel—one another. By focusing its lenses on the unseen world of human interaction, astrology provides that microscope, as it closely inspects the dynamic interplay of individual temperaments.

FIRE, EARTH, AIR, AND WATER

In its analysis, astrology has discerned four irreducible particles of human personality, known as the astrological elements: fire, earth, air, and water. These four elements are called the *triplicities*, so named because there are three astrological signs for each element.

Those born in the Sun-signs of Aries, Leo, and Sagittarius, in the fire triplicity, show a dominant fiery quality in their temperaments, as if kindled by some kind of inner spark. Similarly, the trio of Taurus, Virgo, and Capricorn, in the earth triplicity, is molded by earth, bent on making things real, material, concrete, and eminently useful in the world.

Gemini, Libra, and Aquarius, in the air triplicity, stay aloft in the realm of ideas, ideals, language, and general principles, striving to keep to the high ground of human affairs. Cancer, Scorpio, and Pisces, in the water triplicity, draw forth feeling, affect, and intimacy from their deep emotional wells.

The triplicity *your* Sun-sign is in will introduce you to your dominant element, since the Sun is so tied in with your identity, self-purpose, and will. It will tell you if you predominantly call on fire, earth, air, or water in adapting to the world, especially in your interactions with others. Your Sun-sign element describes your identifiable temperament, your everyday "working chemistry." It is your core substance, the basic stuff of your psychology.

JUNG'S TYPOLOGY THEORY

In fact, the elements in astrology, as indicators of temperament, correspond significantly with a key idea in modern psychology, namely Jung's typology theory, a concept that classifies personality into the following four psychological types:

- the intuitive type
- the sensation type
- the thinking type
- the feeling type

Typology theory is one of Jung's major contributions to the field of psychology. (He also delved into astrology, investigating some 900 charts of married couples in considerable detail. His findings—that there are meaningful, yet acausal, significators of compatibility in the astrological chart—are found in his essay "On Synchronicity.")

While typology theory is not wholly identical with astrology's element definitions, there are enough significant similarities to make a case for comparison. The four psychological types posited by Jung have striking similarities to the temperaments associated with each of the four elements in astrology, as follows:

fire	=	Aries, Leo, Sagittarius
	=	intuition = the intuitive type
earth	=	Taurus, Virgo, Capricorn
	=	sensation = the sensation type
air	=	Gemini, Libra, Aquarius
	=	thinking = the thinking type
water	=	Cancer, Scorpio, Pisces
	=	feeling = the feeling type

Jung called the four psychological types "functions," which they really are, in that we call on them for their usefulness; we rely on them to function in life. They can metaphorically also be called psychological "muscles," for we are strong in them, automatically using them to function capably in the world.

Likewise, the astrological elements also inform our functioning personality, helping us work effectively with life's demands. When we are "in our element," we are functioning well.

Typology theory is used today as the basis for many diagnostic tests in the field of psychology, namely for occupational placement, vocational guidance, personality and relationship counseling, and other practical evaluating purposes.

In astrology, the elements are also useful as a diagnostic tool because they indicate, by way of the dominant element in a chart, what basic psychological function a person relies on to perform well in life.

THE FIRE TRIPLICITY
✳
ARIES, LEO, SAGITTARIUS

Borrowing from Jungian typology theory, then, if you are a fire Sun-sign, you are also an intuitive type, someone who functions in life with flashes of insight. Using spontaneous guesswork, you often "go" on a hunch, or have a sudden premonition; you typically operate by the seat-of-the-pants.

You function largely by instinct, immediately perceiving a situation's inherent possibilities, its unseen potentials—its future—all of which inspire you to act. You also trust that your vitality, charisma, magnetism, and enthusiasm will contagiously inspire others. And they usually do.

Yet, others may perceive you as a risk-taker, impetuous, impulsive, daring—and perhaps even reckless. What they may not realize is that you are simply obeying your "sixth sense," the intuitive knowledge you carry inside, and which you heavily lean on to get through life capably. It is this knowledge, with its sense of prospect, that adds to your well-being and inner security. In Jungian terminology, intuition is your strong, or superior, function.

THE EARTH TRIPLICITY

*

TAURUS, VIRGO, CAPRICORN

If you are an earth Sun-sign, you largely depend on bodily sensation to make your way through life, relying on what is tangible, real, physical, palpable. The known five senses—not the sixth—are your trusted instruments. If you had a sixth sense, it would be common sense. You are reassured by practical and material things, like money, property, worldly status, a steady job. You are the show-me, hands-on, seeing-is-believing kind of person, who needs to know where your next meal is coming from—and how much it will cost.

On the surface, others may perceive you as overly cautious and pragmatic, perhaps slow to act and react and certainly never one to jump into things. This is because of your elemental need to stay rooted in the ground of physical reality—the present. You rely on this "here and now" groundedness for personal well-being, as you must experience the world as having boundary, limit, shape, form, solidity—all of which you mediate through the physical senses. Your strong, or superior function, is sensation.

THE AIR TRIPLICITY
✳
GEMINI, LIBRA, AQUARIUS

If you are an air Sun-sign, you are predominantly a thinking type, good at employing your intellectual skills as instruments of exchange, connection, and communication. Using your mind as your dominant muscle, you rely on its strength to work your way rationally through a situation.

You have the capacity to rise above events by linking past and present into a conceptual chain, giving logical reasons why. In this way, you elevate events—and even people—into abstractions, general principles, and ideals, taking them to the mental plane.

Because of your ability to detach mentally, others may perceive you as somewhat impersonal, even coldly analytical. Still others may characterize you as absentminded, up-in-the-clouds, or preoccupied. However, you are simply adhering to rational patterns, grids, and motifs that comprise your inner world of mental imagery. They are the working diagrams of your thought processes, helping you negotiate your way through life. Thinking is your strong, or superior, function.

THE WATER TRIPLICITY
✳
CANCER, SCORPIO, PISCES

Finally, if you are a water Sun-sign, you are a feeling type, sensing a situation's emotional tone. You rely on hard-to-define "impressions" that are subtly yet indelibly registered inwardly. You are acutely sensitive, seemingly able to pick up psychic vibrations from others, as if tuned in to their wavelengths. (Incidentally, such things as psychic vibrations and wavelengths are very real to you.) You are also highly influenced by your own moods and by shifting sentiments that seem to refer back to the past—even past lives. Life's intangibles deeply affect you.

To others, you may appear irrational or ill-advised, and certainly mystifying in your life decisions. What they may not understand, however, is that you are answering to another voice that stirs your inner world. Your life-actions, in turn, follow that voice's mysterious directives—not outward logic. You rely on the presence of this subtle "inner guide" to cope with events, because it is authentic to you. Feeling is your strong, or superior, function.

INTROVERSION AND EXTROVERSION
IN THE HOROSCOPE

As a further refinement Jung differentiated the four functions with two broad psychological types: the introverted and the extroverted. The introverted type is mainly stimulated and energized by inner, or subjective, experience; the extroverted type by outer, or objective, experience.

Jung called introversion and extroversion "attitudes"—points of view—as distinguished from functions. The two attitudes and four functions combine to fine-tune the personality.

Just as the four psychological functions are related to astrology's elements, the two attitudes of Jungian typology, introversion and extroversion, have a corresponding application in astrology, as follows: The energies of the lower half of the natural astrological wheel belong to introversion; the energies of the upper half belong to extroversion.

The Sun-signs of Aries, Taurus, Gemini, Cancer, Leo, and Virgo, at the lower half of the wheel, are largely subjective in their attitudes toward life.

They reflect a private, internal, personal, self-oriented point of view—in a word, introversion. They seek such things as self-expression and ego identity.

They also represent, by way of the first six houses of the natural wheel, early stages of development that are centered around the inner-directed world of home, siblings, family, and childhood experience.

The Sun-signs of Libra, Scorpio, Sagittarius, Capricorn, Aquarius, and Pisces, at the upper half of the wheel, are largely objective in their relationship to life. They reflect an extroverted attitude that is oriented toward others. Their energies are generally public and external, mainly relationship-centered or societal. In many ways they are also transcendent or supraspiritual—that is, they seek to unite with something greater than the personal self.

They also represent, by way of the last six houses of the natural wheel, late stages of development that are centered around the outer-directed world of partnership, social awareness, professional life, large humanistic concerns, and adult experience.

When we combine the four elements (or psychological functions) with the two attitude types, we refine the personality temperaments even further astrologically, as follows:

SUBJECTIVE ORIENTATION

fire	=	intuition	=	the intuitive type
	+	introversion	=	Aries, Leo
earth	=	sensation	=	the sensation type
	+	introversion	=	Taurus, Virgo
air	=	thinking	=	the thinking type
	+	introversion	=	Gemini
water	=	feeling	=	the feeling type
	+	introversion	=	Cancer

OBJECTIVE ORIENTATION

fire	=	intuition	=	the intuitive type
	+	extroversion	=	Sagittarius
earth	=	sensation	=	the sensation type
	+	extroversion	=	Capricorn
air	=	thinking	=	the thinking type
	+	extroversion	=	Libra, Aquarius
water	=	feeling	=	the feeling type
	+	extroversion	=	Scorpio, Pisces

If you are an Aries or a Leo—a fire sign at the lower half of the natural wheel—you express your intuitive gifts subjectively. You display magnetism, drive, and creativity in intuitive ways but also in ways that put a personal, self-oriented stamp on things: in the case of Aries, by enhancing ego development and establishing self-independence; or, in the case of Leo, through self-expression and putting forth your individual will.

As a Sagittarian—at the upper half of the wheel—you bring visionary fire mainly to societal concerns and broad external issues, seeking an outer, or objective, context for your enthusiasm, ardor, and inspiration. In your ongoing quest for meaning in life, you are spurred by intuition, like Aries and Leo, but you seek a comprehensive answer largely within cultural or collective arenas.

If you are a Gemini—an air sign at the lower half of the wheel—you exhibit a capacity for thinking in mostly personalized, small-scale realms of activity. You are also highly susceptible to personal influences in your immediate environment and are easily swayed by subjective considerations, by what is "in the air." You are mentally impressionable, able to draw in and internalize ideas, usually from a variety of sources.

As an airy Libra, however—at the upper half of the wheel—you seek outer-directed, one-on-one exchanges as the vehicle for your thinking, preferring the fertile ground of another person to pollinate your ideas. As an Aquarian—the most objective of the airy or thinking types—you apply yourself best to impersonal yet all-embracing collective concerns, held mainly in public or group forums, seeking with this an overall concept of truth for humanity.

If you are an earthy Taurus or Virgo—at the lower half of the natural wheel—sensation is experienced mainly on the subjective level. Material objects take on personal meaning and value: in the case of Taurus, existing as virtual extensions of yourself; or, in the case of Virgo, as practical mechanisms for testing and perfecting yourself. For both signs, any possession— a thing, person, job, or the physical body itself—becomes a kind of privatized emblem, imbued with personal significance.

As a Capricorn, on the other hand—at the upper half of the wheel— you apply your earthy, sensate nature to outer-directed goals, seeking status and approval from exterior authority by way of high accomplishment, worldly success, and other external criteria. Your sense of reality itself is defined by your actual professional standing in life, where you can claim "material" ownership of a place in society.

If you are a Cancer—a water sign at the lower half of the wheel—you experience feelings in a deeply personal, internalized way. You are guided by subjective emotions that are largely self-referential. You keep your feelings to yourself and protect them from intrusion by the outside world. Your fluctuations of feeling, or moods, also seem to resonate with vibrations from an enclosed inner space.

As a Scorpio or Pisces—water signs at the upper half of the wheel—feelings take on an external cast. You are swayed by a need for union, for a kind of mystic connection with others. Merging with others, or another, is paramount to your being, whether erotically, in the case of Scorpio, or spiritually, in the case of Pisces.

Your Sun-sign element, along with its subjective or objective component, provides a kind of personality profile, a silhouette of your psychological type in astrological terms. This is by no means definitive, of course, since we have not here explored in any depth a personal horoscope, with its multitude of other factors. However, the same principles of astrology apply in either case.

BALANCING YOUR ELEMENTS

Your working element, as found in your Sun-sign, reveals important psychological truths. It tells you how you work through stress, how you function in the face of it—in short, how you cope with life's demands. Like the personality muscle it is, your working element grows stronger from sheer use and habit.

However, simply *because* we depend on one element so consistently, we tend to become overly dependent on it. Like any favored muscle, it can be overworked, leaving other parts of ourselves undeveloped. Therefore, we periodically need a counterbalancing element for psychological ballast.

Since we automatically "run" to the favored element at the first sign of personal difficulty, we often cling to it for self-identity. If we identify too closely with a strength, ironically, it ultimately weakens us, making us one-sided and eventually lopsided. At such times we must balance our dominant element with another that will refine us—not just define us—so we can become more fully developed as a *whole* person.

For example, if you are a "watery or feeling type," you may, under stress, cry or otherwise easily display a lot of emotion. While this may momentarily help you to cope, it may also be inappropriate or overwhelming to the person you are with. Your superior function, in such a case, is simply an automatic reaction and not useful.

Your outpouring may actually keep you from expressing what you want to get across—what upset you in the first place. It is usually something connected to a past grievance, or the past in general, because you, a feeling type, tend to dwell on these events.

However, if you cannot adequately express in a clear, logical way what is bothering you, neither the situation you are in nor the person you are with will change. The grievous past will stay implacably in the present, with little hope for a better future. Thus, in certain instances in real life, your ordinarily helpful feeling function may actually be a maladaptation, a psychological deterrent to growth.

Similarly, if you are an "airy or thinking type," you may, in the face of a messy "flesh-and-blood" encounter (perhaps from that feeling type you live with), habitually hide behind a book, newspaper, or high-minded principle. Meanwhile, the problem's cause and effect—its past and present—is tied up in a neat little bundle in your head, which you will be glad to unwrap as soon as the other person is ready for some rational thinking.

In this case, even though you are mentally coping with a situation in life, you are not really being receptive or responsive to it. Nor are you offering the other person a creative solution for the future. Your ordinarily helpful thinking function actually serves as a retreat from life and not a true engagement with it, since cause and effect, without a vision for change, is a closed system.

Without emotional receptivity, the possibility for improvement in a relationship, and in yourself, is seriously diminished. In certain instances in real life, therefore, your usual means of adaptation may really be holding you back psychologically, seriously limiting your personal growth and prospects for happiness.

Now, if you are an "earthy or sensation type," you usually alleviate stress in concrete ways, which material life easily obliges you. You may automatically head for the fridge, the store, or work. While the fridge may give you temporary gratification, it may also interfere with other ego gratifications of a more lasting nature. And the trip to the store, while providing you with endless numbers of inanimate "things," may be a substitute for inspired problem solving or meaningful activity. Work too may be another word for drudgery, for being stuck in the present tense without any vision, prospect, or future.

In these instances the physical outlets that normally help you cope may be actual roadblocks to your inner and outer growth, trapping you in matter, so to speak, leaving you immobilized and unable to move forward. By limiting life's interactions to what is strictly tangible, you may be neglecting your capacity for emotional reflection, for example, which is so necessary for change. Or for future planning, where a bold intuitive leap may be called for. There are times in life, then, when your tried-and-true sensation function can actually leave you in a psychological rut.

Finally, if you are the "fiery or intuitive type," you may under conflict or stress head straight for the door, for the road, or for something more "promising." While this may provide temporary satisfaction, it may really be only an impetuous reaction and not a mature response. You view the demands of the present as often confining, and the past seems finished— because your eye is always on the future.

But real progress is seldom achieved without stopping to think, reflect on past errors, and make concrete plans. By dealing realistically with the issues at hand, you have a greater chance to realize proposals, programs, and prospects. Otherwise, like the biblical Ezekiel with his fiery visions, you can end up spinning wheels within wheels, a lone voice crying out in the wilderness. At certain times of life, therefore, your creative fire, vitality, and farsightedness do not serve you well because they leave you burned out psychologically.

In all these instances, what had helped you cope before—whether with fire, earth, air, or water—no longer represents how you prefer to manage from the standpoint of your greater development.

As if by magic, it is at these crucial times that you usually experience "chemistry"—an uncanny fascination with someone else. That other person invariably "shows up" with your missing, or needed, element, and a sudden attraction is formed. You are unaccountably invigorated and enlivened by the experience, awakened to yourself. The entire encounter acts as a catalyst for change, presenting you with a new formula for life. By way of this other person you experience a different, less familiar, part of yourself.

This less familiar aspect of yourself is what Jung called our "inferior" function. In astrology, that unlived part of ourselves—often experienced by way of another person—represents the stirring up of an element that has been dormant. At a particular time of life that element comes to the fore, further integrating the personality.

The "particular time of life" is usually indicated in astrology by a transit, or progression. Each of these terms represents a later position of a planet that affects the birth chart by its impact on a planet in it. While transits and progressions are beyond the scope of this book, these techniques are just some of the myriad ways that dramatic changes in life direction, or changes in perspective, are discerned in astrology.

THE ALCHEMICAL PROCESS

Given the dynamic interplay of astrology's elements as described, we can also say that what we have been calling the "chemistry" of human interaction is really a kind of "alchemy," a process of transmutation, where an element transforms its essential nature when combined with another element.

Actually, alchemy is the forerunner of modern chemistry. Its roots are ancient, originating in Egypt. Like astrology, it found its way into Western Europe by a circuitous path. There, it was practiced from the Middle Ages until the seventeenth century, when it was swept away by the scientific revolution.

The alchemists believed in the unity of all matter. They worked with different mixtures of astrology's four elements in order to produce what they called the "quintessence," a kind of fifth element they believed to be latent in all things, and the substance of the planetary bodies. Their work combined practical chemistry with astrology, philosophy, and mysticism. One of the most famous alchemists, Paracelsus, a sixteenth-century Swiss physician, believed that a person who practices the healing arts should be an alchemist, astrologer, and theologian—so as to tend body, soul, and spirit.

Like the alchemists of old, we can also combine the four elements of astrology—by way of the signs—to see how they interact with each other to produce change. To do this we must set up a kind of chemistry class, exploring and analyzing by pairs the various ways astrology's elements actually impact on each other. In this way you can gain insight not only into your own basic chemistry—your psychological substance—but also that of your "fascinating other."

Staying with the Sun-signs, we will combine the elements two by two (along with their corresponding psychological functions) and begin our chemistry class.

Fire and Earth

Intuition and Sensation

Aries, Leo, Sagittarius ✳ Taurus, Virgo, Capricorn

A fire Sun-sign must often be given shape to its intuitive prospects and daring insights with practical planning, disciplined effort, and tangible results. With an earth Sun-sign—the sensation type—coming into its life, the fire sign will now experience the more pragmatic, realistic side of its own nature and develop new strengths in the process.

The fire sign may feel a loss of "potential" that the earth sign's limitation, boundary, and form will bring, because fire does not like to be contained. But the fire sign's projects and goals enter the realm of concrete possibility now—instead of mere promise—thanks to the solid influence of the earth-sign person, who will make things happen, for real.

What about the impact that fire has on the earth Sun-sign? Fire, by its nature, ignites whatever it touches. By coming into an earth sign's life, the fire sign gives passion, intensity, spark, vision, and enthusiasm to the earth sign's more prosaic view of things.

The fire sign, with its gift of vision, gives a sense of purpose and renewed fervor to the earth sign's labors. Work now becomes part of a larger, more expanded, inspired—and meaningful—life. The present is now more bearable and less burdensome, due to the creative "futurism" that the fire-sign person provides.

But in the chemistry of human interactions, we should remember that proportion, the proper admixture of elements, is all-important. Too much earth on fire can smother it. An overly practical viewpoint often buries intuitive prospects before they even have a chance to catch fire.

Alternately, earth, in its nature, generally perseveres and supports fire's all-consuming spread. But if fire's intuitive prospects are not well contained, all the earth sign's efforts quickly turn to ashes. Too much fire on earth can scorch it, leaving it dry, infertile, and without resources—in a word, depleted.

All the fire Sun-signs are *yang*. They contain penetrating, action-oriented, seeding energies. The earth signs, on the other hand, are all *yin*. They embody receiving, containing, nurturing energies. Because they are so different in their inherent natures, fire and earth signs require a special adjustment to one another—integrating their elements is often challenging. When they blend well, however, they are beautifully balanced, in a *yin-yang* pattern of natural harmony and flow.

Fire and Air
Intuition and Thinking
Aries, Leo, Sagittarius ✸ Gemini, Libra, Aquarius

When a fire Sun-sign meets up with an air Sun-sign, a dynamic, interactive, action-oriented chemistry is initiated because both these elements are *yang*. Since fire, in its fundamental nature, needs air in order to burn, there is a built-in affinity between these two elements.

In this same sense, a fire sign often needs the "thinking" input of the air Sun-sign to keep its hopes and prospects alive. Without air—thinking—to back it up, the fire sign can lose its vitality, its very life force. Intuition can provide the initial spark to get prospects off the ground, but without ideas to feed the fire sign's vision, nothing will really fly.

The thinking type adds perspective to the fire sign's futuristic plans, providing conceptual depth to fire's intuitive sketches. By showing how things evolve from other things and how one step logically follows another, air gives fire dimension, measurement, a sense of the right proportion, thus helping fire intelligently expand its initial design. Air gives the fire Sun-sign clarity of vision because it unites past and present, cause and effect, giving fire the knowledge it needs to make its leap into the future.

In a similar way, fire affects air by stimulating the air Sun-sign's thinking. Fire can change the property of air by forming—and then releasing into the atmosphere—new gases. Inspired, even visionary, thinking is the result, since fire transforms ideas into ideology. It puts heat, ardor, and a sense of purpose into air, setting ideas on fire, so to speak. Fire also frees thinking by sparking creative solutions, stemming from the fire sign's quick insights.

For proper harmony, however, the active *yang* chemistry of fire and air must be carefully blended and balanced. Fire and air combined can also be highly combustible. Too much fire on air can overignite, even inflame it, and cause air to lose its clarity and logic—becoming nothing but "hot air." With too much fire on air, what began as a simple premise can also turn into burning fanaticism, or grandiose, inflated thinking.

In a kind of reversal, too much air can put out fire by a sudden gust of wind, or overintellectualization, blowing out fire's intuitive spark. Too much thinking can often destroy enthusiasm and passion and inhibit progress. If there is too much air on fire—an overabundance of ideas—it can also cause fire to go out of control. Since fire always seeks to expand, if not well-contained it can inflame everything along its path.

Fire and Water
Intuition and Feeling

Aries, Leo, Sagittarius ✳ Cancer, Scorpio, Pisces

When a fire Sun-sign combines with a water Sun-sign, a complex chemistry is formed because, like fire and earth, the differences in their elemental nature are challenging and often difficult to integrate. Water is *yin*, fire is *yang*. Reflective, receptive, and enclosing energies seek to interact with active, penetrating, and expanding ones.

A water sign, with its feeling capacity, brings emotional depth to a fire sign's soaring aspirations. Fire can use water to reflect or look back at the past as a guide to the future. Water can bring to fire a sense of life's subtle nuances and "feeling-tones."

Fire, in its thrust, can often lose sight of such things as responsiveness, nurturing, comforting, and the sensitivity that water can provide. Water puts feeling into inspiration and imbues it with deeper meaning.

Water adds warmth to heat. It provides the hearth in front of the fireplace, the setting and place for a family's emotional connectedness. In this sense, water contains fire, placing it within a shared, encircled context. Within this vessel, fire's incendiary passion can be converted into love. In another sense, however, water's formidable emotional pull can also often restrain or hold back the impetus, initiative, and "heroic" individuality of fire.

A fire Sun-sign has an impact on a water sign in a reverse fashion, whereby the emotions are highly intensified. Fire also provides a sense of purpose, direction, and movement to water's often vague, unfocused impressions. In this way fire can invigorate water, making it percolate with energy.

Intuition and feeling, expressed as fire and water, have something in common. They share a "locale." Whereas sensation lives in the body and thinking dwells in the mind, or brain, the water and fire signs, when combined, connect by way of the heart—through love.

Where love is concerned, the admixture of fire and water is powerful and complex, requiring special handling. Too much fire on water can make it boil; overheated passions easily turn to steam and quickly evaporate. Too much water on fire—as cloying attachment or emotional neediness—douses the flames entirely because above all fire needs freedom.

Earth and Air
Sensation and Thinking

Taurus, Virgo, Capricorn ✳ Gemini, Libra, Aquarius

If we envision earth and air in nature itself, we do not immediately discern a symbiosis. After all, earth is solid and material; we can touch it. Air, however, is utterly invisible. We know it is there, but we cannot really see it. But, if we think about it, all physical, organic life depends on air in some way. Certainly, human beings could not exist without it.

In this same sense, body and mind are profoundly connected yet are vastly dissimilar. So it is with the earth and air signs, or with sensation and thinking as corresponding psychological functions. The mind has a profound influence on the body's health and vitality, and physical well-being plays an enormous role in the state of the mind.

A variation of the mind-body connection is found in the interplay of theory and practice because they too complement, reinforce, and validate each other. Similarly, an earth Sun-sign and an air Sun-sign work hand in hand, creating practical wisdom and the joining of knowledge and experience.

The pragmatic, rooted, task-oriented earth sign is stimulated by the air sign's lofty ideals, ideas, and principles. By applying reason to reality, the air Sun-sign—with its capacity for linking cause and effect—gives the earth Sun-sign an escape from the limiting confines of the present. Earth often feels pulled down, burdened by the world's weight. A thinking type's input can lift the earth sign up to a more elevated plane, removing it from strictly mundane concerns.

An earth sign, for its part, translates an air sign's abstract concepts into real terms, demonstrating to air that all the theory in the world means little if it is not verified in practice. Since an air sign can get lost in the clouds and mental musings, an earth sign brings it down to earth, offering feasible suggestions. The earth sign also brings greater bodily awareness to the air-sign person, who is often not in touch with his or her physical nature.

If there is too much earth on air, however, an air sign feels trapped, bound, and overly restricted by practical considerations. Conversely, too much air on earth inhibits an earth sign's capacity to do things expediently. An overabundance of ideas often runs contrary to the single-mindedness of practical accomplishment.

The earth sign is *yin*; the air sign, *yang*. Their energies are complementary *and* fundamentally different from each other—like mind and body, or theory and practice. This makes integrating earth and air especially challenging, requiring not only adjustment but also imagination because their chemistry is truly a paradox.

Earth and Water
Sensation and Feeling
Taurus, Virgo, Capricorn ✳ Cancer, Scorpio, Pisces

We need only look outside on a rainy day to appreciate water's effect on earth in the natural world. Without water, earth would be dry, infertile, and unable to sustain growth. In a similar way, when a water Sun-sign comes into contact with an earth Sun-sign, it adds emotional support, feeling, and nurturing to earth's productive endeavors.

An earth sign, in its elemental nature, is rooted and grounded. It toils unstintingly at the tasks at hand, complying as best it can to the ever-demanding present. A water sign, with its emphasis on the past, supplies to earth's "soil" the necessary attachment, depth, and enrichment to give the earth sign a sense of continuity and emotional purpose.

If earth without water is an emotional desert, then water without earth is a flood of feeling, an overflow of sentiment without boundary or stability. An earth sign provides a water sign with a sense of practicality, as well as a workable container, or frame, for water's often ambiguous impressions.

Both earth and water are *yin*, pointing to their natural compatibility and mutual receptivity. In their most harmonious aspects, they represent the unity of body and soul. A sensation type needs feeling and emotional connectedness in order to prevent its pleasure-seeking nature from sinking into mere physical indulgence. A feeling type, in turn, requires a solid vessel to hold its watery contents if it is not to dissipate its vast emotional energies.

Too much earth on water, however, stops water's natural flow. Water, after all, can be contained only so much; it must have fluidity, or some form of emotional outlet. If overwhelmed by earth's heavy-handed pragmatism, water simply goes underground; it is repressed, devious, secretive, and deceptive.

Too much water on earth converts to mud, causing the earth sign to sink under water's emotional pull. Earth needs to see results, to make a tangible product of some sort, and to shape something real. If it is mired in the water sign's overly emotional demands, its usual accomplishments will lack clarity, definition, and solid form.

Air and Water
Thinking and Feeling
Gemini, Libra, Aquarius ✳ Cancer, Scorpio, Pisces

Perhaps more than any other combination, the dichotomy of thinking and feeling is most readily apparent in everyday life. To think clearly presupposes the suspension of feeling. Likewise, to feel things completely allows little room for thinking. In the same way, air and water Sun-signs challenge one another because their energies are difficult to integrate.

Yet, it is precisely these differences that make it possible for each to complement the other, where each compensates for the other's lack. An air Sun-sign, living too much in its head, may need to pay greater attention to feelings in order to allow compassion, empathy, and sympathy into its life—to provide the element of water to what may have become a dry and brittle soul.

By the same token, a water Sun-sign, if so caught up in its feelings that it becomes emotionally swamped, may need the detachment, separation, and perspective that the element of air can offer. The *yin* water-sign energies then flow into *yang* air-sign energies, and vice versa.

Water's emphasis on the past can lend depth to air's tendency to consider—often without true reflection and introspection—the past as simply the logical "cause" of the present. On the other hand, the thinking type's capacity to link past and present can actually be the water sign's lifeline, rescuing it from drowning in emotional history.

Too much air on water, however, is inhibiting. The water sign is sensitive, fragile, and impressionable. If its feelings are overintellectualized by the air sign's mental detachment, they evaporate. Water then converts into clouds—by turns moody, dark, and torrential.

If too much water is on air, however, fog results. Thinking is no longer clear or cogent. It is submerged instead in a sea of emotion, unable to come up for air. Air needs freedom to rise above things or to distance itself. If an air sign is inundated by a water sign's engulfing pull, where all thinking drowns, the air-sign person becomes unreasonable, absurd, and argumentative.

In a similar way, if ideas are invested with too much feeling, they turn into dogma, a kind of emotional thinking where feelings become "attached" to concepts, unable to separate from them.

When harmony exists, however, air and water create a serene landscape, where thought and thoughtfulness inhabit the same psychic space. Thinking and feeling, despite their differences, have much to give one another.

THE TRIPLICITIES

We have explored combinations of elements that are dissimilar. Yet we are often drawn to somebody with whom we share the same working element—whose Sun-sign is in the same triplicity as ours. In our interactions with that person, our basic disposition is enhanced and revealed, sometimes favorably, sometimes not.

Fire and Fire
Intuition and Intuition

Aries, Leo, Sagittarius ✳ Aries, Leo, Sagittarius

If two fire Sun-signs are involved with one another, the passions are often quickly ignited, but they are also prone to depletion and burnout. Fire and fire are in a kind of crucible together, with a flame beneath them. As a result, their life together is full of drama, action, drive—all of which are propelled by flashes of intuition that spur them to undertake further projects.

In medieval alchemy, this process of intense burning was called *calcinatio*, the Latin word for calcination, a term that means heating something to an intense temperature until it loses its moisture, reduces down, or combusts. As a metaphor, *calcinatio* stands for a life of passion and engagement as a necessary way to find a person's bare essence, because one's "dross" is burned off in the process.

In astrology, when two fire signs combine, a kind of *calcinatio* occurs. Thus, if the two do not pace themselves carefully, their emotions become quickly exhausted, as they are often expended in the relationship in an intensely blazing, accelerated way. Usually, however, there are enough other elements in each person's chart (by way of the signs that other planets besides the Sun are in) to balance the interplay of fire with fire in the Sun-signs alone.

Fire sign relationships must find ways to convert the incredible life force and power of each of their Sun-sign's fire into suitable form. When this happens, the fire signs together have a great capacity to share a common vision productively. As a team they exhibit enormous courage, energy, and enthusiasm, with motivation to accomplish things.

Two fire signs in relationship are also lively and expressive together, with each sign separately asserting its individuality, independence, and will. They are invigorating and stimulating in their relationship—to each other as well as to others—always aflame with vitality and alive with possibilities. For them, life is one big, creative adventure.

Earth and Earth
Sensation and Sensation

Taurus, Virgo, Capricorn ✳ Taurus, Virgo, Capricorn

Something solid and lasting is invariably formed when two earth Sun-signs come together. As a rule, they like to work jointly toward things that can be pointed to as tangible accomplishments. A trip to the countryside, for example, is not about simply looking at the scenery. Taking along the boat, fixing up the cabin, planting a garden, cooking food on the fire—working concretely on something—more aptly defines the experience. Something "real" must occur, an event in which the senses are aroused, exercised, and fully engaged.

Yet, stopping to admire the scenery—metaphorically speaking—is also essential to living because it allows for dreams and reflections. Two earth signs, therefore, would do well to take time out from their often workaholic, task-oriented tendencies, so their life together does not take on the feel of work, of always having to produce.

In medieval alchemy, this process of concretization was called *coagulatio*, or coagulation. In coagulation, a liquid or gas is transformed into a solid, usually by way of a catalyst. In symbolic terms, *coagulatio*, then, stands for the struggle or difficulty of taking something fluid or formless and giving it a concrete shape. As such, it represents a life of hardship, of constantly grappling with reality, of having to bring things into concrete form.

In astrology, when two earth signs combine, a kind of *coagulatio* occurs. This process of crystallization, hardening, or solidifying, however, can be a two-edged sword. When you concretize something, you also cut short its potential for growth. The relationship, similarly, can hit a kind of psychological rut, where pragmatism rules the day—often at the expense of passion, adventure, and creative risk. However, there are usually enough other elements in each person's chart to mediate the abundance of earth in the Sun-signs alone.

Two earth signs in a relationship have the capacity to shape a solid, good, productive life together. As a team, they exert much effort to achieve the material things of life. In return, they have a great deal to show for it. Life, for them, is about mastering the physical world by "working" it.

Air and Air
Thinking and Thinking

Gemini, Libra, Aquarius ✹ Gemini, Libra, Aquarius

When two air Sun-signs become involved with each other, the proverbial meeting of the minds takes place. Issues, ideas, ideals, principles, and points of view are invariably discussed. They may be disputed, attacked, or mutually agreed on—but they are always in the foreground if the relationship is to "click." Thinking is the relationship's primary means of exchange.

Air signs like to communicate verbally, whether about books, films, art, or language itself, as long as their thinking capacity is engaged. Depending on their educational level, the subject matter they talk about may vary, but their approach to each other is primarily on a mental plane. They talk about their feelings, but with the same dispassion they bring to other matters. In other words, emotional content is generally lacking.

Air, by its nature, seeks to "rise above," to escape to the heights. Similarly, two thinking types prefer to be uplifted in their interactions, to stay aloft in the higher sphere of reason. They tend to keep common matters—even matters of the heart—as impersonal and abstract as possible. In medieval alchemy, this process of elevation was called *sublimatio*, or sublimation. The word *sublimation* stems from the same Latin root as sublime.

In sublimation, a solid material is changed to a gas, or vice versa, without ever becoming a liquid, which symbolizes the emotions, the feeling life. Symbolically, *sublimatio*, then, represents a life of the mind, where the chaos of experience is brought to a more sublime place by being transformed into symbols, concepts, or abstractions. The term *sublimation* was also introduced to psychology by Freud as a process whereby instincts—often unruly or disturbing—are directed into more adaptive, socially accepted, and manageable forms.

In astrology, when two air signs combine, a kind of *sublimatio* occurs. However, if sublimation—in the Freudian sense as well—takes the form of consistently avoiding the blood, sweat, and tears of real emotions, the relationship ultimately withers away. However, there are usually enough other elements in each person's chart to counteract the overabundance of air in the Sun-signs alone.

Typically, two air signs in a relationship have a mentally alive, stimulating, and imaginative life. As a team, they can take flight into a truly liberated state of mind, where they play with ideas creatively, allowing intellectual passion to free their capacity to feel.

Water and Water
Feeling and Feeling

Cancer, Scorpio, Pisces ✳ Cancer, Scorpio, Pisces

The emotions either flow or flood when two water Sun-signs get together. Either way, the relationship never lacks feeling. What it may lack, however, is boundary, since water has no real form of its own: If it is to take shape, it needs some type of containment. Feeling, like water, simply runs away with itself if there is nothing solid to keep it from overflowing.

Water signs, or feeling types, seek to merge with one another, whether emotionally, erotically, or spiritually. As a result, they often "seep" into each other's psychic space, sometimes to the extent that personal identity is submerged. Each is so attuned to the other's feelings that the slightest nuance of sentiment from one causes some sort of emotional ripple in the other. Often because of this, the relationship itself feels tenuous, fragile, and fluid—always seeming to be on the verge of dissolving.

In medieval alchemy, this process of dissolving was described as *solutio*, or solution, where a substance is immersed in liquid until it disintegrates and loses its shape and individual property. Symbolically, *solutio*, then, represents a life of emotional surrender, of the constant breaking down of ego structure, and of the concomitant need for flexibility—simply needing to go with the flow of things.

In astrology, when two water signs combine, a kind of *solutio* occurs. It is experienced through the couple's love for each other, because of its merging quality. In the best sense, it represents a relationship of mutual empathy, kindness, compassion, and sympathy, along with a special appreciation of such things as art, music, poetry, or mystic studies.

But, if the two water signs are immersed too much in one another to the exclusion of individual and separate development, each water Sun-sign ultimately loses its personal identity and feels inordinate emotional dependency on the other. Fortunately, however, there are usually enough other elements in each person's chart to bring detachment, ground, or individual ego expression to the blend of water and water in the Sun-signs alone.

CONCLUSION

Since we have explored each possible combination of astrological elements, our chemistry class is over. But before moving on to the next section of this book, where we will discuss the planets, let us return briefly to our metaphor of alchemy. In early times, much of the alchemical work was about a process of extracting gold from ordinary, even base matter, by way of fire, earth, air, or water in various combinations and by various methods. The process viewed the elements as symbolic agents of change, or transformation.

In modern times, the alchemical work is what we might today call personal transformation, the therapeutic process of turning experience—however difficult, base, or ordinary—into something rich, substantial, and valuable.

By working with the elements in astrology, we bridge two worlds, ancient and modern. In discovering our habitual response patterns, attitudes, and dispositions, we can mine our own substance, bringing to the surface a kind of psychological pay dirt that can help us transform. In essence, we are extracting the gold that has always been there, within us.

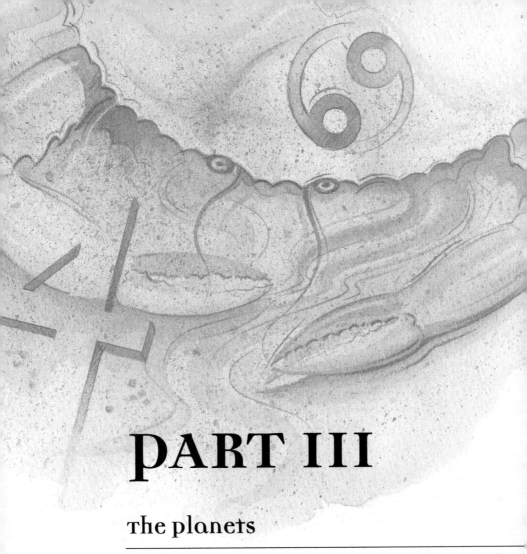

PART III

the planets

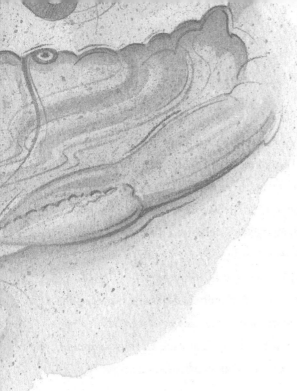

THE MYTHS OF GREECE AND ROME

In telling your story, astrology draws on tales that were first related by others. They are the stories of the gods and goddesses of ancient Greece and Rome, for whom the planets are named. In antiquity, the deities were believed to animate all parts of the natural world, but they were also envisioned up in their heavenly home in the sky—or high on Mount Olympus, its lofty equivalent.

Their stories are of a time and place. But they are also timeless and everywhere. They are the myths, told and retold all over the world, in a multitude of ways, always and forever. Although related by way of the lives of the Immortals, they speak of eternal human verities.

Their motifs are birth, death, love, betrayal, cunning, wisdom, aggression, and more—all of which are drawn from the deep well of human experience. They speak about the family and its complex dynamics, about mother, father, sibling, child. And also about the hero or heroine in each of us. The villain, cheat, and coward too.

In astrology, the myths—and their motifs—are told by way of the planets, who speak for the deities. The planets in astrology are symbols for the universal themes that are lived out in myths. In the horoscope, they are the "life principles," the prime movers in the drama of human experience.

The planets clearly visible in the sky are Mercury, Venus, Mars, Jupiter, and Saturn. As we have stated, in ancient Greece and Rome, these—along with the Sun, Moon, and stars—were believed to reflect the divine light of the gods and goddesses as they illuminated the heavens.

Several centuries after the Age of Antiquity had passed, however, the three new planets (all found with the aid of the telescope) were also named after deities of the Greco-Roman pantheon. They are Uranus, Neptune, and Pluto, and are called the outer planets in astrology because of their great distance from the Earth.

In the chapters that follow, we will explore all the planets—ancient and modern—along with their myths as they pertain to the human story.

PLANETS IN SIGNS

We have described how only *one* planet, the Sun, when donning the "costume" of a sign, will express itself in that sign. We have done this by taking the Sun through all twelve signs of the zodiac—just as it does in its yearly round. In the process we also touched on the Sun's meaning in astrology, describing it as a kind of extension of yourself—a projection of your intent and will—emanating from the center of your being.

In the next chapter, we will explore the mythic symbolism of the Sun itself as a way to understand how its depictions in mythology resonate with its astrological meanings.

But what about the other planets? They also appear in the horoscope, each one placed in a sign. After all, every planet in astrology (as in the sky) is positioned somewhere along the zodiac; so they must, like the Sun, have a sign attached to them. Like the Sun, each planet's sign is also determined by where the planet was located along the zodiac when a person was born. The astrologer integrates *all* the planets—each in its respective sign—in interpreting a chart.

In your personal chart, every planet would be placed within a pizza-pie segment of the wheel in its proper sign (where it was along the zodiac when you were born)—just as we placed the Sun in its pizza-pie slice of sky in our earlier exercise. (And, as noted, the sign a planet is in describes how that planet expresses its life principle.)

Without the benefit of a personal chart, however, you cannot determine which signs your planets are in. (An ephemeris would also provide you with a list of all the planets' signs on your date of birth, but as a non-astrologer, you would not ordinarily have access to such a specialized book.) You know your Sun-sign only—as most people do—but not necessarily your Moon-sign, Mercury-sign, or Venus-sign, for instance.

For those who *do* know their planetary signs, they can consult the countless books in astrology, colloquially known as "cookbooks," which devote themselves solely to taking *each* of the ten planets through *all* the twelve signs—just as we have done in chapter 4 with the Sun alone. However, since many readers may not be familiar with their personal horoscope, it would not be useful to follow a cookbook format here. Neither would it fulfill the purpose of this book, which is to present basic principles that can be applied to all horoscopes, including your own.

For this important reason, therefore—regardless of how familiar you are with the sign positions of the planets in your natal chart—it is essential that you understand the core meanings of the planets of astrology *in and of themselves* before they are "dressed up" in signs. In chapters 4 and 5, you were given extensive information about signs in general. After learning what each planet stands for in its core meaning, you can then "attach" sign qualities to them (using the analogy of verb and adverb, respectively).

RULING PLANETS

The core meaning of one particular planet, however, is especially relevant to you: the "ruling planet" of your particular Sun-sign. That planet is a vital part of your personal astrological profile because it is connected to your Sun—the symbol of your identity, purpose, centrality, and self-intention in life.

We have already pointed out how sign, house, and the planet ruling them form an astrological triad, sharing a common symbolic base (we used the example of the sign of Virgo, the sixth house, and their ruler, Mercury, to illustrate this point). The Sun in Virgo is here both subjected to and imbued with the power and influence of Mercury; it effectively defers to Mercury because Mercury is the ruler of the sign of Virgo. In this instance the Sun—the essential you of the horoscope—must somehow merge its inherent meaning with Mercury's inherent meaning.

As we explore each of the planets in the following chapters, you should pay special heed to *your* ruling planet (the planet ruling your Sun-sign), integrating its symbolism with that of the Sun's. In this way, you will enrich and expand your understanding of your Sun-sign, even beyond what you have learned about it in chapters 4 and 5.

PLANETARY CYCLES

Before we discuss the planets, however, there is some additional information you should know about planets: They constantly move. The planets in your horoscope at birth, however, are momentarily "frozen" in place. It is as if a circular snapshot of all the planets in their respective sign positions along the entire zodiacal belt (above the horizon and below the horizon) was taken and preserved for you to keep. That snapshot is your natal horoscope.

To use our usual example: You may have been born when the Sun was in the thirty-degree segment (the pizza-pie slice) of the zodiac called Virgo. *Your* Sun (from *your* horoscope), therefore, is *in* the sign of Virgo—you are a Virgo. As we have seen in chapter 4, however, the next month, the Sun travels into Libra on its yearly round. This does not change your natal horoscope; you are still a Virgo, even though the Sun has moved into another sign.

Regardless of where the Sun was at *your* birth, the Sun itself continues to travel through all twelve signs of the zodiac over the course of a year, staying in each sign for about one month. (By dividing the 365 days of the year equally by twelve, we obtain about thirty days per sign, or one month.)

In your natal horoscope, all the other planets are also fixed in place, remaining in their respective signs. They become *your* Moon, *your* Mercury, *your* Venus, and so on. But each planet, like the Sun, keeps moving in the sky—each at a different rate, depending on its distance—always from Earth's perspective. The farther the distance a planet is from Earth, the slower it appears to us to move.

The astrologer interprets your horoscope based on the positions of *all* the planets, including the Sun, at that set moment of time—your birth. However, the astrologer also takes into consideration *later* positions of planets as they keep moving around the zodiac over time. These later positions are then compared with the set positions of your natal horoscope to see how the "moving" planets impact on the "immobile" planets in your horoscope (if they form aspects to one another, for example).

In astrology, the moving planets affecting the set planets in the natal horoscope are called "transits." Transits are the stock in trade for the working astrologer; they are used for forecasting, studying character development, and a variety of other purposes.

The Moon, which moves quickly from Earth's perspective—since it is relatively close to us—takes about a month to travel through all twelve astrological signs. (Again, your Moon at birth will stay where it was in your birth chart—in the sign it was in at the time. In astrological terms, you would then say your natal Moon is *in* that sign, just as you would say your natal Sun is *in* a sign.)

If we traced the Moon's movement around the twelve signs of the zodiac over a month's time, we would see that the Moon stays in a sign for about two and a half days. (By dividing the thirty days of the month equally by twelve, we obtain two and a half days per sign.)

The amount of time it takes a planet to travel around the entire zodiac is called a "planetary cycle." According to the length of its cycle, a planet spends a certain amount of time in a zodiacal sign. The Sun's planetary cycle is one year; the Moon's is one month.

Jupiter, however, which is farther from Earth, appears—from Earth's perspective—to move much more slowly around the zodiac than the Sun or Moon. Jupiter takes twelve years to travel through the twelve signs of the zodiac, remaining in each sign for a year. (By dividing twelve years equally by twelve, we obtain one year per sign.)

Saturn, even farther than Jupiter, takes some thirty years to travel around the zodiac, remaining in a sign for about two and a half years. (By dividing thirty years equally by twelve, we obtain two and a half years per sign.)

The three outer planets are great distances from Earth. They therefore appear to stay in a particular sign for a much longer period of time. It takes Uranus, for example, eighty-four years to travel through all the signs of the zodiac. It stays in one sign for seven years. (By dividing eighty-four years equally by twelve, we obtain seven years per sign.)

Neptune takes about 164 years to make a complete cycle of the zodiac. It spends about fourteen years in a sign. (By dividing 164 years equally by twelve, we obtain fourteen years per sign.) Although Pluto takes about 248 years to complete its cycle, because of the nature of its orbit its time in a sign can vary from twelve to thirty-two years.

THE GENERATIONAL PLANETS

In astrology, the outer planets are also called "generational planets." This is because they influence a whole population in their long-term effects, since they remain in one sign for many years. Pluto, for example, was in the sign of Scorpio from 1983 through 1995. Everyone born during that period has Pluto in Scorpio in their horoscope.

Scorpio was a powerful sign for Pluto to be in, since it rules Scorpio. In its astrological meaning, Pluto symbolizes the principle of death and regeneration; it is a planet that ultimately transforms in radical ways. Pluto in the sign of Scorpio, therefore, demonstrated how sexuality (Scorpio) could be a destructive force in the world (Pluto), affecting a whole generation of people.

Those were the years that saw the terrible devastation brought on by AIDS and other sexually transmitted diseases. Now that Pluto has moved out of its own (ruling) sign, where its force was especially strong, astrologers believe the planet's severe Scorpionic effects will gradually subside.

The boxes on the following pages provide a listing of the signs the generational planets were in during the twentieth century, as well as where they will be in the early decades of the twenty-first century. From these listings, you can trace where *your* outer planets were when you were born—that is, what collective "wave," or spirit of the times, you came into being with.

For example, before Pluto was in Scorpio, it was in the sign of Libra (from 1971 to 1984), the time of the so-called "sexual revolution," which had a profound global effect on cultural lifestyles and gender roles. In particular, it was an era when traditional relationships (Libra) underwent radical change—virtually "dying" in the process (Pluto) before they could be transformed anew.

URANUS IN THE SIGNS FROM PISCES THROUGH AQUARIUS

URANUS IN PISCES

April 1919–August 1919
January 1920–April 1927
November 1927–January 1928

URANUS IN ARIES

April 1927–November 1927
January 1928–June 1934
October 1934–March 1935

URANUS IN TAURUS

June 1934–October 1934
March 1935–August 1941
October 1941–May 1942

URANUS IN GEMINI

August 1941–October 1941
May 1942–August 1948
November 1948–June 1949

URANUS IN CANCER

August 1948–November 1948
June 1949–August 1955
January 1956–June 1956

URANUS IN LEO

August 1955–January 1956
June 1956–November 1961
January 1962–August 1962

URANUS IN VIRGO

November 1961–January 1962
August 1962–September 1968
May 1969–June 1969

URANUS IN LIBRA

September 1968–May 1969
June 1969–November 1974
May 1975–September 1975

URANUS IN SCORPIO

November 1974–May 1975
September 1975–February 1981
March 1981–November 1981

URANUS IN SAGITTARIUS

February 1981–March 1981
November 1981–February 1988
May 1988–December 1988

URANUS IN CAPRICORN

February 1988–May 1988
December 1988–April 1995
June 1995–January 1996

URANUS IN AQUARIUS

April 1995–June 1995
January 1996–March 2003
September 2003–December 2003

NEPTUNE IN THE SIGNS FROM CANCER THROUGH AQUARIUS

NEPTUNE IN CANCER

July 1901–December 1901
May 1902–September 1914
December 1914–July 1915
March 1916–May 1916

NEPTUNE IN LEO

September 1914–December 1914
July 1915–March 1916
May 1916–September 1928
February 1929–July 1929

NEPTUNE IN VIRGO

September 1928–February 1929
July 1929–October 1942
April 1943–August 1943

NEPTUNE IN LIBRA

October 1942–April 1943
August 1943–December 1955
March 1956–October 1956
June 1957–August 1957

NEPTUNE IN SCORPIO

December 1955–March 1956
October 1956–June 1957
August 1957–January 1970
May 1970–November 1970

NEPTUNE IN SAGITTARIUS

January 1970–May 1970
November 1970–January 1984
June 1984–November 1984

NEPTUNE IN CAPRICORN

January 1984–June 1984
November 1984–January 1998
August 1998–November 1998

NEPTUNE IN AQUARIUS

January 1998–August 1998
November 1998–February 2012

PLUTO IN THE SIGNS FROM CANCER THROUGH CAPRICORN

PLUTO IN CANCER

September 1912–October 1912
July 1913–December 1913
May 1914–October 1937
November 1937–August 1938

PLUTO IN LEO

October 1937–November 1937
August 1938–February 1939
June 1939–October 1956
January 1957–August 1957
April 1958–June 1958

PLUTO IN VIRGO

October 1956–January 1957
August 1957–April 1958
June 1958–October 1971
April 1972–July 1972

PLUTO IN LIBRA

October 1971–April 1972
July 1972–November 1983
May 1984–August 1984

PLUTO IN SCORPIO

November 1983–May 1984
August 1984–January 1995
April 1995–November 1995

PLUTO IN SAGITTARIUS

January 1995–April 1995
November 1995–January 2008
June 2008–November 2008

PLUTO IN CAPRICORN

January 2008–June 2008
November 2008–March 2023
June 2023–January 2024
September 2024–November 2024

sun and moon:

Archetypes of Light

THE SUN

In most cultures, old and new, and from places that encompass the world's geography, images of the Sun as a life-giving, divine source of power are widely prevalent. Even before the Sun's centrality in our planetary system was scientifically known, people had an intuitive sense of the Sun's supremacy in sustaining life on Earth.

In the Americas, Sun-designs have been found on buffalo skins from the Blackfeet civilization of the Great Plains, suggesting the Sun's role in some sort of sacred rite. The Incas of ancient Peru built elaborate gold-covered temples in homage to the Sun, who they worshiped as a god. And as far back in time as prehistory, cave drawings discovered in Asia and Africa show human and animal figures with Sun-disk heads, which seem to endow the figures with special powers.

In early Christian iconography, the head of Christ is also often depicted with a nimbus, a radiant circle of light behind or above it, the Sun-disk here representing the theme of Christ's spiritual power and divine origin.

In whatever fashion the symbolism of the Sun is depicted in different cultures, beliefs, and historical times, its bright, golden, circular form conjures up the idea of a great, energetic force influencing life. Its strength and vitality seemingly emanate from its fiery center.

The Sun in Astrology

In astrology, the Sun's meanings resonate with the time-honored imagery just described, but predominantly as they relate to the individual psyche. The Sun is about *your* centrality—the vitality, strength, and firepower that propel you forward in life. It is the light, or spirit, that dwells within you, emanating from your center. Its source may, indeed, be divine, but its expression is inherently human.

The astrological glyph for the Sun, ☉, depicts the circle of spirit; the dot within it represents the infinite source at the Sun's center.

The glyph is also a smaller rendition of the circle of the horoscope itself as it traces the Sun's path around the zodiac—a circle that we earlier described as the "road of life," as the ancients called it. In chapter 4, as we took the Sun through the zodiac, we spoke of it as your guide and alter ego on this road; this is because the Sun stands for *you* in your greater purpose as you travel along *your* road of life. It is your story, first and foremost, that is told within the circle of the horoscope. You are its central character.

The Sun in astrology signifies your integral, individual self as you strive for completion, fullness, and wholeness as the seasons of your life progress. The dot within the circle in the Sun's glyph also represents the central mystery that is you; within that mystic center is your life's purpose, or "plot," which is still unfolding.

The Sun as Light-Bringer

In whatever symbolic or pictorial form it took through the ages and in various cultures, the Sun was also always revered as the light-bringer. As an archetype it also stands for consciousness itself—the dawning of awareness. In your chart the Sun casts its illumination and light wherever it is placed.

Each day originates with the Sun; it defines the day's opening, its conscious awakening. The Sun is also a symbol of genesis. In chapter 4, we saw that the sign of Aries, at the start of spring, is also about beginnings, about the initial spark of creation and the awakening of life force and energy. In astrology, the Sun is said to be "exalted"—brought to its highest power—in the sign of Aries.

If your Sun-sign is in Aries *or* Leo (since the Sun rules the sign of Leo), your Sun is "dignified," imbued with extra prestige and authority. These are considered to be strong Sun-signs, designating a high amount of initiative, self-assertion, self-expression, confidence, and willpower.

As a metaphor, we often speak of the Sun as being "reborn" each day as it rises out of the darkness. Similarly, we say that we are also reborn with the morning Sun as we emerge from the dark night of sleep. Today, of course, this is purely a metaphor. We no longer strictly wake up to the Sun and go to bed at its setting; we have become accustomed to electricity and clocks.

Indeed, we hardly take note of the Sun's daily journey: its rise at the eastern horizon, its climb to the top of the sky, and its westward slide into the earth or the sea. But to our early ancestors, the Sun's daily rebirth and its semicircular arc in the sky were truly awesome.

Before electricity, people's experience of light itself came from the sky—the greater light from the Sun, the lesser light from the Moon and stars. The daily arrival of the Sun, a great ball of blazing light rising out of sheer darkness, was a perennial source of wonder. The Sun's daily journey across the sky resonated with the miracles of birth, death, and resurrection in human life—along with the growth cycles of nature.

The Sun Depicted in Myth

As reflected in countless Sun-myths, early humans envisioned the Sun as a magnificent, heroic figure, born from a great, good mother, who, by giving birth to the Sun-hero, participated in the process of providing food and sustenance to the world.

In mythic iconography, earth and water were connected to this great mother, since the Sun-hero was seen as emerging from the land or the sea—as if from the womb. Earth and water were perceived as feminine, dark, and mysterious yet creative and life-giving.

Astrology is still wedded to this ancient verity. The earth and water signs (Taurus, Cancer, Virgo, Scorpio, Capricorn, and Pisces) are feminine, or *yin*; they are described as containing and receiving fertile energies. In delineating your chart, for example, the astrologer highlights these qualities in discussing *how* a planet (or planets) in these signs expresses its inherent nature.

In recurring myths, the Sun-hero—after being born from the great mother—leaves her to go on his quest, reaching his highest visibility and strength at the top of the sky. As the Sun touches the high heaven, however, his fiery energy combines with air and then explodes as thunder and lightning and bursts open the clouds. Rain falls, penetrating the earth and filling up the oceans, providing the land and sea with the fertilizing seed of life. With this, the Sun's inseminating power became personified as a great father, who could regenerate all of nature.

In mythic iconography, fire and air were connected to this great father, since the Sun-hero (now the Sun-king) was perceived as a seed-giver, impregnating the land and replenishing the seas. Fire and air were imagined as masculine, phalluslike, and active—and, like earth and water, part of the creative, life-giving process of nature.

In astrology, the fire and air signs (Aries, Gemini, Leo, Libra, Sagittarius, and Aquarius) are similarly masculine, or *yang*. They are described as dynamic, penetrating, and generative energies. The astrologer highlights these qualities in discussing your planets in fire and air signs.

Yin and Yang

We should point out now that the terms *yin* (feminine) and *yang* (masculine) as used in astrology are meant as energy principles, not gender descriptions. For example, an Aries woman is of the feminine gender, naturally. But her Sun-sign energy is *yang*, "masculine," thrusting, active, motile. As an Aries, she will also be fiery, assertive, and initiating in expressing her Sun's will.

In the same way a Cancer man's Sun-sign energy is *yin*, "feminine," receptive, supportive, holding. Although he is masculine in gender, he is nurturing, protecting, and sensitive in expressing his Sun's will.

Because of the common confusion between gender and the energy principles of active and receptive, in modern astrology the less "loaded" terms, *yin* and *yang*, are preferred over feminine and masculine. As a matter of fact, nothing in a horoscope indicates one's gender.

But the planets in astrology, as told through their myths, *are* gender-specific. The Sun, in its symbolic life principle, is masculine, fiery, and *yang*. The Moon, which we will soon discuss, is feminine, watery, and *yin*. Again, *both* men and women have the Sun (and the capacity for heroism, strength of purpose, and individuation) and the Moon (the capacity for empathy, receptivity, and emotional connection) in their horoscopes.

The energy vibration of *yin* and *yang* reverberates through all of astrology—as we have seen in our study of the natural wheel. As light-giving hero or life-giving king, for example, the Sun may be portrayed as a masculine figure, but it can express itself in both *yin* and *yang* ways, as can all the planets in the horoscope.

Since astrology draws so heavily on mythic themes, we can also see how the dynamic interplay of *yin* and *yang* is also mirrored in the Sun-myth. It concludes, as the day does, with the setting Sun. As it sinks into the land or sea, the Sun is mythically envisioned as being received anew by the great mother.

From this simple observation, the human family saw the Sun-hero connecting heaven and earth—*yang* and *yin*—in the world of all observable nature. Psychologically, this gave reassuring continuity to life on a day-to-day basis. The deeply embedded perception of the Sun's outer journey still sits at the core of human consciousness as we make our own heroic round from dawn to dusk each day.

The Sun's Night Journey

We have traced the Sun-hero's outer journey across the semi-arc of the sky, bringing light and consciousness to the world on his daily climb. In astrology, the Sun's range of meanings in the horoscope is also extracted from this

Sun-myth: purposefulness, individual will, a sense of separate selfhood, and heroic strivings in general.

Accordingly, when *your* Sun (the "you" in the horoscope) is at the "top of the world," you are productive and energized, casting no shadows; you feel at the height of your powers. You have a sense, also, of your own "kingship"—of inner authority, centrality, and strength of purpose (all of which you express through the qualities of your Sun-sign).

There are times in life, however, when your Sun feels sunk into oblivion, as if swallowed up in darkness, not unlike the Sun-hero as he plunges down at dusk into the mouth of the sea. These are the times when you are psychologically in the dark, in the grip of despair or depression. You lack vitality, will, and self-purpose, as symbolized by the Sun.

This psychological plunge into darkness is also captured dramatically in myths, which always draw their contents from the great reservoir of human experience. There is a body of myth that pertains to the Sun-hero's "night journey," of his time in the shadowy realms that lay beneath the visible horizons; typically, these stories tell of perilous struggles with sea monsters. In countless such tales, the hero is swallowed alive, entombed in the "belly of the beast." In the well-known Bible story, for example, Jonah is wholly ingested by a whale, only to be released after kindling his faith.

Just as the Sun-hero does in his setting, we are similarly drawn—often compelled—to embark on our own kind of underworld voyage, exploring our own psychic depths. Whether through astrology, psychology, spiritual practice, or any other process of inner work, we are taken at such times into the deep interiors of our being, as we delve into our past, family life, personal history, and dreams.

THE MOON

In astrology, this inner journey is symbolically associated with the Moon, for the setting of the Sun coincides with the onset of night. At night, it is the Moon who rules the sky.

The translucent, indirect light of the Moon has a soft, silvery glow. It is subdued, dreamy, and diffused, evoking in us a feeling of serenity. We like to gaze at the Moon; we attach our dreams and fantasies to it.

Countless poems and songs have been written about the Moon's ability to stir and touch us at our emotional core. Its elusive, mysterious light causes us to long for something profoundly inexpressible—yet primal and compelling. Its magnetic draw seems to pull us inside ourselves, connecting us to our inner world.

The Moon is endowed with a quality we can only call "soul." Its nocturnal aura sets a certain mood that absorbs, fascinates, and mystifies us. While spirit, like the Sun, seems to rise or sink, soul permeates; it seeps into the deepest crevices of our being.

The Moon in Astrology

Soul is the key word for the Moon's meaning. The astrological glyph for the Moon, ☽, is the crescent, the curved line that signifies soul, just as the Sun's glyph, ☉, the circle, represents spirit. Soul and spirit are the animating principles of life—one *yin*, the other *yang*—because without soul and spirit, physical matter is devitalized or dead. Together, *yang* Sun and *yin* Moon exist in a dynamic yet harmonious relationship, since each has within it a vibration that flows into the other, like the breath of life itself.

The Moon epitomizes the receptive *yin* energies, since it receives, holds, and reflects the Sun's light. In the night sky, we can observe how much of the Sun's light the Moon bestows by way of the Moon's phases. (Later in this chapter, we will take you through the Moon's monthly cycle, exploring each of its eight phases.)

In keeping with the Moon's rulership of the maternal sign of Cancer, in astrology the Moon also encompasses the full range of meanings that surround the complicated phrase "to mother." Like the Moon itself, the word *mother* stirs up deeply rooted feelings. Mother was our first love; how she reflected our love back to us forms the psychological matrix of our emotional life.

Mother is primary to all experience. There is no one who has not had a mother, whether good, good-enough, bad, or absent. The Moon in the horoscope, primarily by the sign it is in, reflects how you relate to all that the word *mother* implies: home, family, the past, roots, memories, and the complex emotions that go with all these.

In your personal horoscope, the sign the Moon is in indicates how you envisioned your mother and all she represents—again, whether she was good, bad, or indifferent. If your Moon is in an earth sign, for example, you may see her as pragmatic, down-to-earth, and sensible. But on a "soul level," you may also perceive her as cold and austere—too busy, perhaps, with tasks to sustain your emotional needs.

Other astrological factors that come into play in weaving together the cluster of emotions around your Moon (and the word *mother* in general) are the aspects your Moon makes with other planets, the transits to your Moon at various times of life, your Moon's house placement, and a wide variety of advanced technical considerations.

In the sum of all these parts, however, the Moon in your chart reflects your internalized mother image (which may or may not mirror your actual mother). It will express your innate capacity for emotional response, nurturing, support, and protection. How do you mother, or take care of yourself? How do you nurture—or fail to nurture—others?

Is your internal mother image an overprotective, limiting, and fearful figure who restricts your self-development? Or a narcissistic, insatiable one, hungering for attention? Or a neglectful, abusive, or unavailable one who offers no emotional peace or contentment? Can you return "home" to yourself for comfort, safety, protection, and love? Are you your own good mother?

These are the kinds of questions the astrologer will explore with you by way of the Moon in your chart, making use of the tools of the trade just mentioned: signs, aspects, transits, house placements, and more.

The Moon and the Physical Body

We are all familiar with the Moon's tug on the sea, which causes the tides to change. But the Moon also tugs on the waters of our physical body, causing our emotions to change. When we are emotional we cry, secrete, perspire, and salivate; our blood itself is stirred. There is something deeply instinctual about all this wetness, something involuntary, automatic, visceral, and uncontrollable, like the emotions themselves.

In astrology, the Moon is similarly connected to our instinctual, emotional life—our unconscious reflexes—in contrast to our conscious will, purpose, and intention, as represented by the Sun. The Moon signifies the land of night, which can be dreamy, soothing, and romantic but also shadowy, dark, and disturbing. The night often stirs up irrational terrors and fears, unsettling memories, and nightmares.

Like the emotions it tugs on, the Moon also fluctuates to show different faces. Unlike the Sun, which is always a bright, golden disk, the Moon's
shape is changeable. It begins as a thin, silvery sliver of light, and as it waxes,
it culminates in a voluptuous roundness. It begins to wane, gradually disappears, and seemingly retreats into its own darkness, only to reemerge. All
of this takes place in a period of about a month (twenty-nine days, twelve
hours, forty-four minutes, and twenty-eight seconds to be exact).

By observing the Moon's monthly cycle, early humans soon connected
it to nature's fundamental rhythm, which was echoed in the natural
rhythms of the physical body and the human life span itself. This common vibratory pattern, similarly described in lunar myths from different
cultures and times, was observed in the Moon as a beginning (waxing), culmination (fullness), and winding down (waning).

In its crescent shape, the Moon, as it began to wax, was often envisioned in myth as a maiden, or virgin, young and full of promise, beginning
her course of life. The full Moon, round and ripened in its imagery, was
imagined as a woman in her maturity, as mother, pregnant female, or a
fully blossomed, opened lover.

As the Moon began to wane, it was perceived as shriveling, as in old
age. Its decrease in shape came to symbolize the crone, or wise old woman,
experienced and knowledgeable in the ways of life—or, in other stories, as
the vengeful witch or the embittered woman.

And as the Moon closed down in utter darkness, disappearing from
the sky entirely, it seemed to die. But in the dark of the Moon, an inner
process of renewal also seemed to be taking place—the sowing of a new
seed of life, sprouting again as the crescent.

As reflected in their Moon-myths, early humans observed this same
threefold process in all of nature: the planting of a seed, its growth and

maturation, its eventual return to the earth, and its regeneration. The Moon, in its cycle, and Mother Nature, in her cycle, were envisioned as following the same pattern.

A woman's biology itself was also seen as relating to the Moon's cycles: menstruation, conception, pregnancy, childbirth, and menopause. The mood shifts, emotional changes, and powerful feelings that these bodily processes engendered in women also added to the Moon's association with the maternal aspect of the feminine motif.

Astrology is attuned to the myths of old, as we have already seen in our discussion of the Sun. As in the Moon-myths, the symbolism of the Moon in astrology is connected to the physical body not only as the seat of instinct but also in its fertile aspect. The Moon is exalted, brought to its highest power, in the earthy and physical sign of Taurus. Taurus's *yin* nature is maternal, like Cancer's; it will hold, endure, preserve, and protect. It is also a sign linked with great procreative power. Taurus's symbolic animal, the bull, which was domesticated in early agriculture, figured prominently in ancient fertility rites, often held amid the furrows of freshly plowed fields.

As stated earlier, the glyph for Taurus, ♉, depicts the bull's head and horns. But the glyph is also a pictorial representation of the Moon's full and crescent shapes, further amplifying its exaltation in Taurus. In the glyph for Cancer, ♋, the crescent and full Moon shapes are also pictorially incorporated.

Soul and spirit, crescent and circle, are combined in both Taurus's and Cancer's glyphs, describing the symbolic link between the Moon and the Sun. Despite the fact that we see the Sun by day and the Moon by night, neither is ever "alone" in the sky. They are always in a relationship, as seen in the phases of the Moon. The Sun and the Moon are part of a pair, which together provides the world with light: the Sun by direct, radiating glare, the Moon by reflection or mediation.

Each month, the Moon's phases are visibly played out in the night sky. Up or out there, the Sun and the Moon, in their relationship, are in a kind of cosmic dance, first joined at the new Moon (when the Sun and the Moon are aligned), then facing apart at the full Moon (when the Sun and the Moon are opposed), then back together again, their rhythm resonating with the pulse of life itself: birth, maturity, decline, death, and regeneration.

The following thumbnail sketch will illustrate how the dance of the Sun and the Moon has meaning that you can apply in practice to your life and activities. You need only look up at the night sky in any month of the year and think symbolically, staying attuned to the Moon's threefold motif: beginning (waxing), culmination (fullness), and winding down (waning). By doing so, you can place yourself in harmony with the Moon's phases and join in the dance.

The Moon's Monthly Cycle in Your Life

Once a month, if you look up at the night sky, you will see the thin crescent Moon emerging from darkness. It looks like this: ☽.

At this stage of the Moon, if you are undertaking something new, it is generally a good time to begin, although you may feel tentative. If you have already begun something—a project, job, or relationship—you may not yet have a sense of the whole picture, which may add to your uncertainty. But you *will* have a sense of its potential, of the promise inherent in its beginning, which will spur you on. You are still green and untried. However, with the crescent Moon, faith is in the air; it is just not backed up by experience.

Three or four nights later, if you look up at the sky, you will notice how the Moon has waxed. When it reaches its first quarter phase, it will look like this: ◑.

You have just had your first experience and it has "broken you in"—because it feels like a crisis. You must overcome the novice's hesitation you may have initially exhibited. In a new relationship, you may experience that first major disagreement; ditto for a new job or project.

At this phase of the Moon, you test your resolve to go forward. If you begin something at this time, it may feel as if you have entered an arena where you need to prove yourself through some action. Your efforts may be met with a sense of challenge.

When the Moon is *almost* full, it is called gibbous (meaning convex). It appears about a week after the new crescent. As the last stage of the waxing Moon, it looks like this: ◑.

You now have a sense of accumulated experience; since overcoming your initial reluctance and its accompanying crisis, you are committed to your tasks, job, project, and relationship. But you may also be feeling overwhelmed by the responsibilities any or all of these entail.

At this phase of the Moon, it is a good time to review and revise, as well as fill in last-minute details; this is also the time to take special care of your health. If you begin something new at this stage, you may inherit a full workload.

The full Moon appears in the sky about a week after the first quarter Moon. And it looks like this: ○.

Whatever you began earlier is now seen in its entirety. It is a time of illumination and realization; for better or worse, you have the full picture of things. Whatever potential existed at the beginning is now fulfilled, or at least defined.

At this stage, you can reap your rewards or simply bask in the light of your accomplishments. Your project, job, or relationship has reached its maturity.

But because the Moon has culminated, it is also at the start of its waning period. Thus, whatever you have achieved from the start will ultimately be transformed. If you begin something new at this phase of the Moon, your awareness of self, others, and the situation at hand will be at peak level; you will walk in with your eyes wide open. However, your accumulated experience is particularly invaluable now, since change is inevitable.

As the full Moon wanes, it enters the next phase, which, as noted, is called the gibbous Moon. Astrologers, however, call it the "disseminating" Moon. Its image is the reverse of the waxing gibbous Moon; it looks like this: ◑.

This phase is the first stage of the wisdom path of your Moon-journey, which is to teach, communicate, and share what you know—to disseminate knowledge. Although the path now leads inward, there is still plenty of light with which to illuminate others. In your job or project, you are a mentor; you are also learning to delegate responsibility to others.

In your relationship, you now share with your partner a legacy of experience—including hard lessons, stories, sorrows, and tales. If you have children, you should impart what you know. However, anything new you take on at this stage may necessitate *your* having to listen, observe, and learn, because you will be coming in near the end of a project.

About a week after the full Moon, you will notice the waning last quarter Moon in the sky. Its image is the reverse of the waxing first quarter Moon; it looks like this: ◐.

Symbolically, by the time of the last quarter Moon, you are seeking meaning to life. At this phase, you are also about to cross a threshold into an interior realm. The impending darkness may feel like a crisis, as it tests your capacity to leave the light. Overcoming your reluctance will ultimately lead you to a hidden treasure: your inner self.

In this same sense, a project, job, or relationship has deepened by now, having been enriched by time, experience, and learned wisdom. Similarly, if you begin something new at this stage, it will call on your concentrated depth and good counsel.

Three or four nights later, if you look up at the sky, you will see the crescent Moon again, its image now reversed. Known traditionally as the old crescent, astrologers call it the "balsamic" Moon; it looks like this: ◐.

At this phase, the light of the Moon has greatly decreased; in a few days, it will narrow into utter darkness. This is a good time for solitude, which is not the same as loneliness. You have the chance, at the balsamic Moon, to find those places in yourself where you had earlier tucked away your dreams. In rediscovering them, the faith you had at the beginning, with the waxing crescent, can be rekindled and renewed, since life's experience has deepened you.

At this stage, a project, job, or relationship must also have meaning and depth, or you will forsake it; the same is true for anything new that you start.

Two weeks after the full Moon, the night sky will show no trace of the Moon. This is called the dark of the Moon, or the new Moon phase. Its schematic drawing looks like this: ●.

If the new crescent Moon symbolizes birth, then the new Moon is the time of conception. And, although we have placed the new Moon phase at the end of this section, it is symbolically the true beginning of the Moon's monthly cycle because the Moon is conjoined with the Sun at this stage.

It is a time when spirit and soul unite, seeding something new in life—expressed as the birth of the new crescent.

The new Moon phase is a time for planning, finding a way to realize those dreams, hopes, wishes, visions, and fantasies you imagined at the old crescent phase. The Sun, signifying your will, and the Moon, signifying your emotions, are locked in a symbolic embrace at this time of the month. And whatever they conceive together "in the dark" of the new Moon will "come to light" at the full, when they stand apart and face each other once again.

Mercury:

The Wings of Thought

THE STORY OF HERMES

Once upon a time (as told in a Homeric hymn of Greek antiquity), a secret liaison took place in a dark cave on Mount Kyllene in Arcadia. A lesser goddess of the night sky, called Maia, and the great Olympian sky-god, Zeus, made love. From their union, a baby boy was born; he was called Hermes.

In folklore, some believed that Hermes's mother was merely a mountain nymph; others said she was the daughter of Atlas, the mighty Titan who alone held up the arch of the sky in the West. Still others have placed Maia as one of the Pleiades, the cluster of stars sometimes called the seven sisters. In his book *The Gods of the Greeks,* classical scholar Carl Kerényi suggests that Maia might have been the primal goddess, Night, herself.

Whoever Hermes's mother was, this much is known from the Homeric hymn (where the most detailed story about her survives): She had to remain deeply hidden within the recesses of her cave, alone with her newborn baby, fearing that her liaison with Zeus would be discovered. Zeus had a wife. And not only was Zeus's wife, Hera, famous for her jealous rages, but she was also queen of heaven, making her powerful in her own right.

Hermes was born early in the morning. However, from the moment of his birth, he did not like his lot in life: to be stuck in a cave deep in some remote mountain, living alone with his mother who would only leave the cave when night fell. He knew that his father was not just a god but the great god Zeus, king of heaven. Why, then, thought Hermes, should he and his mother be secreted away while his father was living it up on Mount Olympus?

It also bothered Hermes that his father was solely surrounded by his Olympian family, in particular by Zeus's other offspring—Hermes's half brothers and sisters—who were counted among the blessed. One of them was Apollo, the golden Sun-god and Zeus's favorite son. Apollo, like Hermes, was not born of Hera, yet *he* had been given a seat of honor at the palace of his father.

Hermes could not imagine spending the rest of his life cooped up and in the dark. At only a few hours old, he was already bored. It was still day, and his mother was hidden in the back of the cave. Curious to know what the world outside was like, he climbed out of his cradle.

The first thing he saw was a large tortoise. What an ingenious creature, he thought. Relying on his own ingenuity, Hermes lured the tortoise inside the cave, killed it, scooped out its body from the shell, and strung seven strings of sheep gut across its opening to invent the lyre. By noon, Hermes was happily singing and plucking on the instrument.

Then he grew hungry. So he stole out of the cave again, this time prowling and lurking around like a thief. As he wandered about, the Sun was beginning to set. Suddenly Hermes came upon a large herd of cattle that belonged to Apollo. The baby decided to steal them.

Not wanting to be caught, he devised a clever scheme. He separated out fifty head, and drove them *backward* toward his cave—so their hind hooves were in front, and their forehooves were behind—making it look from their tracks like they were going *toward* Apollo's pasture. Hermes also fashioned a pair of large sandals for himself, made out of twigs and leaves to obliterate his tracks. When an old farmer caught sight of what he was doing, Hermes cajoled him into silence.

It was almost the next morning when Hermes stopped to let the cattle graze not far from his home. He made a fire, slew two of the cows, and roasted their meat. Instead of eating it, he divided the meat into twelve equal parts, offering up one piece and paying homage to each Olympian separately: Zeus, Poseidon, Hades, Hestia, Hera, Ares, Athena, Apollo, Aphrodite, Artemis, Hephaestus—*and himself*. Hungry as he was, Hermes then buried the sacrificial meat, as was the custom when making an offering to a deity. Having performed the ritual, he now considered himself a god among the Olympians, and an equal among equals.

By nightfall, Hermes slipped quietly back into his cave, slid into his cradle, and snuggled deeply into his baby blanket. He lay there, pretending to be asleep, hugging his lyre like a teddy bear. But his mother, coming out of hiding, was not fooled; she immediately challenged him about his misdeed.

Hermes said: "Do you think I was born yesterday? I am not going to let us both cower here in a dark cave, completely ignored, while the Immortals cavort merrily on Mount Olympus, receiving all kinds of gifts and prayers. My father must give me the same honor he gives to Apollo, or I will rob Apollo again to get what is coming to me."

Meanwhile, Apollo, searching for his missing cattle, had already spoken with the old farmer, who told him about seeing a boy wearing strange-looking sandals and driving fifty cows backward. Using a series of signs and omens, Apollo discovered where the boy was, stepped into Maia's secret cave, and illuminated it with his golden aura. Hermes lay innocently curled up in his cradle, hiding his eyes from the divine glow, as if he had just been awakened from sleep.

But when Apollo accused him of thievery, Hermes sat up, protesting, suggesting that Apollo was picking on him, a mere infant. Apollo, knowing the truth, proclaimed Hermes a liar and branded him the prince of thieves for all time.

But beneath his outrage, Apollo was secretly charmed by the infant's audacity. He picked the baby up, whereupon Hermes defecated on the god's golden palm. He also sneezed in Apollo's face, acting like a real baby who suddenly had been taken over by all sorts of bodily functions.

In exasperation, Apollo carried Hermes away, taking him directly up to Mount Olympus. There, he deposited Hermes on Zeus's lap, and made his case before his father to obtain justice. Although the all-knowing Zeus recognized Hermes at once (and knew of everything that had transpired between him and Apollo), he pretended not to know his child—not only because he feared Hera but also because he was embarrassed about his tryst with a mountain nymph. Still, he was delighted with the baby, thinking that the boy would make a good messenger, since his mind was so swift and his way with words so convincing.

Hermes accused Apollo of picking on him, and pleaded with Zeus "who was, after all, his rightful father"—to defend him. Zeus burst out laughing.

It would have been heartless of Zeus, who was known to love his children, to deny his paternity, especially since the baby was precocious and cunning. To settle the matter, he ordered Apollo and Hermes to reconcile.

And, refusing to punish an infant, Zeus commanded Hermes to return the cows to Apollo. Obeying, Hermes led Apollo to where he had hid the cattle.

While Apollo herded them, Hermes nonchalantly played a melody on the lyre, singing a paean to Apollo. Apollo was enchanted as the instrument's tones pierced his heart with joy and love. He had never heard anything that delighted him more. Compared with the magnificent sound of the lyre, the theft of fifty cows now seemed unimportant. Apollo promised Hermes anything he wanted in exchange for the lyre.

Hermes gave Apollo the lyre. In return, his older brother offered many gifts, including fame and wealth (plus the fifty cows). But perhaps the greatest of all was the job he was given of *psychopomp* (meaning "escort of souls"). He could now guide souls into the underworld—and return safely. Apollo also arranged with Zeus for Hermes to be counted among the Immortals, with the office of divine messenger.

Zeus, in turn, gave Hermes a special helmet not only to protect him in all kinds of weather but also to serve as a symbol of the mind's conscious component (a messenger must be alert to things). He also added to the hat wings for speed and mobility, and gave Hermes a pair of winged sandals and a herald's wand, the caduceus, which became a healing rod.

With his newly acquired gifts, Hermes, now the official messenger-god, could freely weave in and out of three separate domains: the upper world of heaven, the mortal realm, and the underworld. And in recognition of his swiftness and acuity, Hermes also came to symbolize for the Greeks the realm of the mind itself: logic, ideas, speech, oral and written communication—and, most important, the mind's ability to "connect" things. The mind is also the body's messenger, instantaneously relaying thoughts, instructions, responses, impulses, and reflexes back and forth through the various paths of the nervous system.

MERCURY

The Romans later modeled their messenger-god, Mercury, on Hermes, giving him identical attributes, as well as the winged props of helmet, sandals, and caduceus. In astrology, the planet Mercury, named for the same Roman god, is also about the quicksilver, agile, "mercurial" way of the mind—its swift ability to string words together into speech and ideas. The mind, like Mercury, is also a deceiver; it is cunning, clever, a player of tricks, and a master of disguises. It can hide a thought, as well as reveal it.

The mind spans—in an instant—past, present, and future. It weaves in and out of three separate domains (the mortal plane, underworld, and higher sphere), just as the messenger-god does.

On the mundane level, the mind functions as ordinary thought, permitting a person to make idle conversation, gossip, and trade; to speak about everyday events, the time, weather, latest news, facts, and figures. This is the mind's mortal aspect, which deals with the present of regular life, as well as with the world of "matter."

Yet the mind also has a deeper layer, a kind of underworld, or "soul" life. Beneath the light, bright, upper surface of everyday language is a darker, less revealing place within the mind's interior. There, hidden shades of meaning exist, giving ordinary language a subtext of feeling, of such things as subtle impressions, emotional tones, memories, associations, vague sensations, and unconscious thoughts. The inner mind also exhibits richness of texture, nuance, shadow, and coloration. This is the aspect of the mind that draws on the resources of the past, on its timeless but also personal legacy of human experience.

Yet another level of the mind is a kind of higher mind, a guiding spirit that propels the mind toward greater consciousness and a sense of purpose in life.

In the darkness of his cave, Hermes sought a connection to his divine origins; as a result, he was prompted to leave its safety to explore life's prospects, to find something for himself. He wanted to make his life meaningful, to unite with something larger than what had been given to him. Ultimately, through his efforts he was offered a useful role to play in life. This is the aspect of the mind that envisions future possibilities.

MERCURY IN ASTROLOGY

In astrology, Mercury encompasses—and connects—these three levels of mind, symbolized in the story as heaven (spirit), the mortal realm (matter), and the underworld (soul). The glyph for Mercury, ☿, pictorially depicts these domains: the circle of spirit, the cross of matter, and the crescent of soul.

Mercury's caduceus, the winged staff with two intertwined serpents, also contains the cross, crescent, and circle in its configuration. As the modern symbol for the medical profession, it represents healing. However, as Mercury's healing rod, it also suggests the connection between mind and body in healing, each influencing the other.

Mercury's rulership of the mentally versatile, quick-thinking air sign of Gemini and the health-conscious, self-perfecting earth sign of Virgo similarly reflects the mind-body duality symbolized by the caduceus. However, Mercury's greatest strength lies in the mind's power. It is exalted—brought to its highest power—in Aquarius, certainly the most rational and mentally inventive of all the signs.

If you are an Aquarius Sun-sign, it is likely that you were born with Mercury in the sign of Aquarius, since the planet Mercury can be no farther than twenty-eight degrees of celestial longitude from the Sun. (Your

Mercury might also be in the neighboring signs of Capricorn or Pisces, depending on your personal horoscope.) However, if you are an Aquarius Sun-sign with Mercury also in Aquarius, your astrologer will most likely rate mental skills and intelligence high on your list of traits.

Mercury's proximity to the Sun also means it is seldom visible in the sky (a half hour before the Sun rises or sets, and then only a few times each year), because it is obscured by the Sun's radiance. This resonates with the story of Hermes and Apollo: the baby secreted in a cave, and bright Apollo (often associated with the Sun in myth) up above with Zeus. But as are all myths, the story is archetypal: It reflects a universal human situation and illustrates the complexity of the sibling relationship.

Mercury's meanings in astrology also include a sibling motif (echoed in the planet's rulership of Gemini, the sign of the twins). By way of Mercury such themes as sibling rivalry, the favored child, the significance of birth order—and the various tricks, pranks, and devious schemes employed among siblings, as they vie for family position—are explored in the horoscope. Who is the "golden" child in your family, for example? Which sibling obscures the other? Who is teamed with the "disadvantaged" parent? How do you share with your brother or sister? The older sibling? The younger? Do sibling issues affect your adult relationships? How?

The sibling archetype can also stand for your own inner sibling, or twin—a part of yourself that is obscured, neglected, ignored, or secreted in darkness. Or a part of you that is childlike, creative, inventive, curious, adventurous—and demanding of attention, identity, and recognition. Which twin do you show to the world? Which one do you hide?

Mercury as an archetype is also the divine child that dwells in all of us. Described in Jungian psychology as the *puer aeternus* (Latin for eternal boy) or *puella aeterna* (eternal girl), the divine child is resurrected each time we marvel, wonder, or delight in a baby—because it reminds us of life's perpetual renewal and its potential. The Christian image of the Christ-child evokes this archetype, as do miraculous-birth stories in other religions because conception itself is a kind of miracle—divine and mysterious. Conception also means idea, suggesting Mercury's connection to the mind.

Psychologically, there is another side to the *puer* or *puella* motif that concerns someone who is a perpetual child. He or she tends to live a kind of provisional life, dreaming up a lot of creative projects and flying off on a variety of tangents but never landing on anything substantial. This is also the person who seldom commits to someone or something, flitting from one thing or relationship to another—not unlike Hermes obliterating his tracks, or paying homage to *all* the deities.

On a more positive note, the *puer* or *puella* personality is often found in artists, musicians, poets, and other creative people who are able to tap into their imagination, cleverness, and wit to make something tangible, like the lyre. When these people appear childish, immature, and undeveloped, others often readily forgive them—as Apollo forgave Hermes when he played the lyre—because of their talent, originality, and inventiveness.

Another facet of Mercury's rich symbolism is the motif of the trickster, magician, or illusionist, as well as the thief. For three weeks, three or four times a year, the planet Mercury moves "backward" in the sky—like Apollo's cattle. This is due to the speed of Mercury's orbit around the Sun relative to the Earth's, an illusionary effect similar to being in a faster-moving train running parallel to a slower-moving train: One appears to be moving backward relative to the other. This seemingly backward motion of a planet is called a "retrograde."

During the retrograde periods of Mercury, astrologers have consistently noticed that such things as mail, telephones, faxes, computers, and other such instruments of communication seem to work less well, or actually break down more often than at other times of the year. It is a time when the "mortal" or material domain of Mercury is not functioning at optimal level. The god seems to be playing tricks on the real world.

In astrology, a retrograde period of Mercury also signifies a good time to look within, to examine events, people, and other matters in your life. Like Hermes escorting a soul to the underworld, you can use this time to guide yourself into your own psychic depths to explore the shadows. For example, you may want to review a past action, attitude, or behavior in a more contemplative way. Or you may wish to revisit a decision you had arrived at too hastily. In general, a Mercury retrograde period is a time to reflect and reconsider.

Apollo branded Hermes the prince of thieves. But Hermes stole the cattle to gain an advantage—not to possess. In the same way, the mind is often used to outsmart or deceive in order to advance one's position. The mind also crosses boundaries, like a thief—just as Mercury crossed over and back again from sky-world to mortal-world to underworld. In ancient times, the god was actually associated with crossroads, a place where people would congregate to chat, gossip, and trade goods and information. The crossroads were also a place where thieves lurked.

Wherever there are two, and a connecting principle, making three, we find Mercury. He of all the deities was able to span three worlds—while inhabiting none. We encounter Mercury figures in everyday life, in such roles as mediator, merchant, negotiator, guide, interviewer, liaison, spokesperson, gatekeeper, fixer, coordinator, matchmaker, and, of course, messenger.

Mercury is also the actor or actress in us, able to take on different roles, to cross over from one realm to the other: The theatrical two-faced mask (one face laughing, one face grieving) is an apt representation of Mercury's versatile nature.

Mercury, then, is as varied, resourceful, quick, deep, and complex as the human mind. He is very much a part of our will, consciousness, and self-identity, as represented in astrology by the Sun—and in the story, by Apollo. Along with the lyre, he has given us delight, daring, a sense of wonder, and the remarkable gift of inventiveness itself.

venus and mars:

Love's Tug of War

VENUS

Of all the deities of ancient Rome, Venus is perhaps the most familiar. Images of the love goddess, shapely and voluptuous, are prevalent, from the armless Venus de Milo statue to Botticelli's equally famous painting, *The Birth of Venus*—in which she is seen emerging from the sea, a giant seashell behind her. Even without an image of her in front of us, Venus is evoked whenever we see beauty, which always attracts us.

Why? The answer lies in the compelling nature of Venus, for she symbolically touches something in us that we can only call our aesthetic sense. It is something that restores—or perhaps reinforces—our own internal balance, making things feel "right," in proper harmony; it profoundly satisfies us. When we perceive it in art, design, music, poetry, architecture, dance, science, mathematics, or even in the grace of an athlete, we feel moved to utter the word *beautiful*. When we meet up with it in another person, we feel moved to utter the word *love*.

Love, the gift of Venus, is one of the central mysteries of life. Like beauty, we are deeply drawn to it but are not really able to define it—except that, like beauty, it gratifies us at our very core. Love's compelling nature also makes us want to express over and over its power and mystery, as if to release its hold on us. The countless revelations about love in songs, poems, movies, plays, books, stories, operas, and soap operas attest to this.

Love may be a singular experience, but there are many different kinds of love: maternal love; erotic love; platonic love; newfound, young love; old and well-worn love; sisterly and brotherly love. For some, there is love of country—patriotism—which is a kind of abstract, paternal love. And there is love that is pure devotion.

There is also demonic love. You can also love pain, conflict, suffering, addiction—things that are harmful. You can love power, wealth, possessions, and passionate causes. The list is as long and varied as love itself.

Love, however, is always "directed." It must go toward an object, a person, place, thing, or idea. The object can exist in reality, or as a fantasy, but it is still an object—it exists as a "thou" to your "I." The emotion of love itself is highly subjective, but it is always attracted to, or projected onto, something outside yourself. You cannot love without something, or someone to love, because love is about relating. It is focused on the other.

Venus in Astrology

"Relatedness" is precisely what Venus stands for in astrology. She represents the binding energy that connects the person to the loved other and vice versa. She is the embodiment of the *yin*, feminine, receptive principle in its attracting, engaging, and embracing aspect. (As we have seen, the *yin* Moon, the maternal face of the feminine, carries a different set of attributes from Venus, although there are some subtle similarities.)

In her capacity to relate, Venus represents in astrology such magnetic characteristics as charm, grace, glamour, artistry, sociability, sexual attraction, sensuality, and, of course, love. She is pleasure-giving, aesthetic, and appreciates material goods, beautiful objects, and other things of value.

As a component of her *yin* nature, she also stands for that part of our psychology that allows us to be emotionally penetrated—where we are open to the other. She permits us our human capacity for relationship, and, with this, she provides a sense of completion, unity, balance, and equilibrium.

She also represents that part of us that is psychologically vulnerable because our protective, self-defending armor is pierced when we open ourselves to another. In this sense, Venus is also where we have a chink in our emotional armor.

The glyph for Venus in astrology, ♀, is the same as the universal sign for female. It depicts the circle of spirit placed above the cross of matter. Renowned astrologer Alan Oken in his book *As Above, So Below* compares Venus's glyph with the Egyptian ankh, which stands for the vitality of life—the universal spirit (circle) manifesting into matter (the cross).

Venus's rulership of both earthy Taurus and airy Libra reflects love's range, as love is both physical and mental. We love with the mind, as well as the body; each is a catalyst for the other. If the mind is turned on, the body responds in kind; if the body is turned on, the mind follows suit.

In astrology, Venus is exalted—brought to its highest power—in the spiritual sign of Pisces. This points to the kind of love that we had referred to in our discussion of Pisces in chapter 4 as agape, the Greek word for selfless love. At best, selfless love is devoted to service to others; at worst, it can describe someone who loves too much, who loses all sense of his or her personal needs when in a relationship.

In working with Venus in your horoscope, the astrologer explores relationship issues with you. Do *you* love too much? Do you lose personal boundaries? Or, on the contrary, are your emotional borders so restrictive that others cannot enter? The different ways you relate, especially in matters of the heart, are found by way of Venus, primarily by sign—but not exclusively so, since love is never that simple.

Venus in Mythology

Venus's mythic predecessor was the Greek goddess Aphrodite, with whom she is equated. In the creation of the world as told by the Greeks (and depicted by Botticelli), Aphrodite emerged full-blown from the sea. As we saw in the Sun-hero myth, the sea was envisioned as the womb of the Great Mother, who gave birth to the Sun each day. In Aphrodite's sea birth, then, she is the personification of fertility.

As soon as Aphrodite stepped out of the sea and onto the land, grass grew and the earth began to blossom. The three graces—Radiance, Joy, and Flowering—greeted her. The goddesses of the seasons, called the Horae, dressed her in beautiful garments and danced happily around her. The animals and birds followed along, and the fish rushed through the streams to keep up with her. In this rich imagery, we have a sense of the goddess as bountiful, creative, and life-enhancing.

All of this expresses the power of love. It makes things flourish. It imparts vitality to everything it comes in contact with. When we are touched by Venus, we are filled with the joy and abundance of life around us. Everything is awakened, enlivened, onrushing, and teeming with activity.

Venus attracts, arouses, and motivates us, filling our lives with fertility, radiance, and color. Her power is the power of nature itself in all its fullness.

Everything in nature, however, contains its opposite as well—its shadow side. Love, like nature itself, can also be destructive, chaotic, and disturbing. In the many stories, poems, and recitations about her, Venus showed that she could be jealous, possessive, vain, petty, deceptive, rivalrous, and a liar—all in the name of love.

In the name of love, Venus had many affairs—despite the fact that she was a married woman. Her husband was Vulcan (called Hephaestus by the Greeks), the lame god known for his craftsmanship. As god of the forge, Vulcan fashioned the various props the deities used to implement their powers—thunderbolts, tridents, breastplates, arrows, helmets, and shields. His pairing with Venus symbolized the marriage of craft and beauty, underscoring Venus's connection to art and aesthetics.

THE MYTHOLOGY OF VENUS AND MARS

One of Venus's most passionate affairs was with Mars, the ruddy god of war and battle. It mattered little to these two ardent lovers that Venus was married. As a matter of fact, when Vulcan caught them in flagrante delicto (literally "while the crime is blazing"), he enmeshed them with an iron net and called on all the gods and goddesses to witness what was going on. (The female deities stayed away; the males went to gawk.) The lovers, inseparable, continued (love knows no bounds). The gods merely laughed at the sight. (Mercury, boundary-crosser and cheat that he was, told Apollo he would gladly change places with Mars.)

In the psychological sense, like Venus and Mars enmeshed in their bed, love and war are also often entwined. We speak of "winning" someone's love, for example, and crudely, of "sexual conquest." Even more crudely, our most hostile four-letter word refers to sex.

Through the ages, duels and battles were fought for love. And certainly, such things as love of country, family, God, values, and ethnicity have inspired people to go to war, even to die. Love, like war, stirs the blood. In many ways, like Venus and Mars, they are two sides of the same coin—one *yin*, the other *yang*—joined by a common passion.

Mars in Astrology

Where Venus was described as receptive, attracting, and relating in her *yin* nature, Mars is said to be penetrating, active, and driving—*yang* in his nature.

Mars, in his capacity to assert, represents in astrology such dynamic characteristics as decisiveness, initiative, bravery, energy, boldness, and the competitive spirit in general. He is also unafraid to break new ground, fight for justice, and, of course, go to war. His shadow aspects are aggression, combativeness, destructive rage, rashness, and invasiveness.

As a component of his *yang* nature, Mars also stands for that part of our psychology that penetrates, which has the capacity to assert itself on another—to pierce defenses. And if Venus is the principle of relatedness, that is, inviting the other in, Mars is the counteracting principle—the willingness to "take the dare," to accept a challenge fearlessly. Mars presents himself as the "I" to Venus's "thou."

The glyph for Mars in astrology, ♂, is the same as the universal sign for male. It depicts the cross of matter (slightly modified in modern usage) over the circle of spirit. Astrologer Alan Oken, in *As Above, So Below,* describes the glyph as Mars's shield and lance, as well as the sexual symbol of male virility and procreative powers.

Mars's rulership of fiery Aries and its corulership of watery Scorpio reflect the broad range of Mars's highly passionate nature. Aries, as a sign, is quick, impatient, headstrong, and heroic. Scorpio is powerful, sexual, intense, and emotionally smoldering. The elements of fire and water, each in their own way, also "charge up" and "feed" the emotions.

In astrology, Mars is exalted—brought to its highest power—in the hardworking, practical, disciplined, and ambitious sign of Capricorn. This suggests that the warrior god does best when he is put to constructive purpose, with an attainable goal and a sense of accomplishment, since the sign of Capricorn encompasses these qualities.

In working with Mars in your horoscope, the astrologer explores the various avenues at your disposal to deal with your aggression, anger, and passion. Do you rage and act out rashly when you are frustrated? Do you displace your anger onto others? And finally, how do you turn your drives and impulses into constructive endeavors?

The Mythology of Mars

Mars, like Venus, was a Roman deity. In ancient Rome, he was second in importance only to the chief god, Jupiter. In ancient Greece, however, Mars's predecessor, Ares, was not highly worshiped. There, he was solely a battle-god and not very well liked. Ares's shrines were few in number, situated mostly in Thrace in the northeast outlands of greater Greece. The people of Thrace were considered rough and raw-edged, even barbarous, fighting simply for the sake of fighting. The Greeks, on the other hand, saw themselves as fighting only for a just cause.

For example, Ares sided with the Trojans in their war with the Greeks, who had the goddess Athena on their side. Athena was noted for wisdom, cool thinking, strategy in battle, and a dispassionate ability to fight for a high principle (for example, justice). Her rational attributes epitomized the Greek ideal. Ares, by comparison, was considered a hothead, a bully, even a thug.

To add to the embarrassment, Ares was the son of the principal Olympians, Zeus and Hera. His parents disliked him intensely, considering him rude, unruly, ill-tempered, destructive, and quarrelsome—a kind of physical brute. He was also highly emotional and a whiner. Some stories say that Zeus deeply despised him, wanting little to do with him; other versions say Ares was born from Hera alone, without benefit of Zeus's seed, signifying that he was cut off from a relationship with male authority.

There was a side to Ares, however, that *was* extolled by the Greeks: his passionate heart, which gave him fierce courage. He was also admired for his fiery leadership, which the Greek poet Homer had to acknowledge was what spurred the Trojans on to battle.

These were the more positive attributes of Ares that ultimately found their way into the Roman pantheon, where, as Mars, he became a dominant god, sharing power with his father, Jupiter—Zeus's counterpart in Rome. As a son, then, Mars developed strength and authority in his metamorphosis from Greece to Rome; he "grew up" along the way.

The Children of Mars and Venus

In his mythology, Mars was a son, warrior, and fervent lover. But he was also a devoted father. He sired more than twenty children. With the greatest love of his life, Venus, he fathered five of them. Their names in Greek were: Eros, meaning desire; Anteros, meaning desire reciprocated *or* desire unmet; Phobos and Deimos, meaning fear and terror; and Harmonia, or harmony.

In the metaphor of the children of Mars and Venus, and what each of their names represents, we are presented with the range and variety of emotions that are spawned in a romantic, sexual, or otherwise deeply felt relationship—since each sibling, as in any family, is an offspring of intimacy. And, as in any family, each sibling is unique despite being born of the same parents.

Eros, or desire, is connected to the psychological principle of libido, or life force. Desire is a powerful trigger for the discharge of libido, providing the impetus that moves it outward—usually toward the desired object. Without Eros, we would lack passion for someone, something, or for life itself. It is an energy, or instinct, that is sexual, but not exclusively sexual; Eros is creative, spiritual, and aesthetic, as well as biological. It is a kind of charged energy that propels us forward.

Anteros, Eros's brother, is seen in myth as a kind of part-brother, or aspect of Eros. Anteros's name is ambiguous: It can mean consummated desire or reciprocated desire; in some stories, however, Anteros is also seen as unrealized desire, or even as the avenger of slighted love, suggesting the negative force that can be unleashed by rejection, inhibition, or the frustration of desire.

With this last aspect of Anteros, libido energy is directed inward. When we are depressed and immobilized, for example, it is often because our libido has fixed itself on a particular complex dwelling in the psyche, tying up energy otherwise available for outer life.

Interestingly, Eros, like his father, also underwent a kind of metamorphosis in his development: Eros became de-eroticized, so to speak. He became sentimentalized by the Greek poets, who gradually envisioned him as a fair-haired, handsome, winged youth, absently and randomly dispensing love by way of his bow and arrow.

In Roman mythology, when Eros was known as Cupid or Amor, he had essentially lost his divine rank—and his intense, erotic desire nature—although he was still associated with love. Today, of course, Cupid is portrayed as a cute, asexual baby boy who surfaces on February 14, the feast day of a martyred Christian saint, Valentine. A custom was initiated in the Middle Ages on St. Valentine's Day to send love notes, since his feast day was also believed to be the beginning of the mating season for birds (Cupid had wings). All this is certainly a far cry from Eros's early role of charging up libido!

Those who have given themselves over to love have met up with Eros in some way, as well as his brother Anteros, through desire reciprocated, consummated—or unmet. In astrology, usually by way of the angular relationship (the aspects) of Venus and Mars in a chart, the many faces of desire are examined, exploring the ways, whys, and wherefores of erotic love. How you deal with unrequited love is also looked at by way of Mars and Venus—based on how they interact with one another, whether by sign, aspect, element, modality, or any number of other astrological factors.

Fear and terror, the brothers Phobus and Deimos, are also born of the union of Venus and Mars. It is said that these brothers always accompanied Mars in battle, shrieking, going berserk, and generally leaving havoc in their wake; as such, they are truly components of war and strife.

However, among lovers, fear and terror can also rear their ugly heads. If we feel threatened or attacked at our emotional core, for example, fear and terror often cause us to lash out defensively at a partner. As by-products of an intense love, and as brothers to desire, they can wreak havoc in our lives as well.

Psychologically, fear and terror are instincts that spur us to fight or flee. When these instincts surface in a relationship, we can succumb to them and retreat. Or we can overcome fear and terror through struggle and engagement, remaining to hammer things out and resolve crucial issues. But if we find ourselves fighting the proverbial battle of the sexes, fear and terror will surely serve as foot soldiers in an ongoing conflict, perpetual allies in a rancorous war that ultimately destroys a relationship.

In astrology, Venus and Mars in a chart indicate what happens when love and passion unite. For some, this union gives birth to fear and terror, causing lovers to flee or retreat from commitment. Often, however, desire—which emboldens us—supersedes fear and terror. And if desire is reciprocated, the last child, harmony, can come to be.

In myth, Harmonia was the apple of her father's eye, the favorite of all his children. Known as "the uniter," she was irresistible in her beauty, truly her mother's child. Mars adored, honored, and protected her. Her grace, serenity, and tranquillity seemed to calm his warrior's heart. This tale illustrates that when love brings forth harmony, even Mars, the fierce and terrifying god of war, is tamed.

But perhaps it was the Latin poet Virgil who really said it best:

> *In hell, and earth, and seas, and heaven above,*
> *Love conquers all; and we must yield to Love.*

Jupiter and Saturn:

Voices of the Father

A STUDY IN CONTRASTS

In old astrology texts, Jupiter was known as the "Greater Benefic," a bringer of good fortune, increase, and expansion. Saturn, in turn, was called the "Greater Malefic," bringing bad fortune, decrease, and restriction. In a horoscope, Jupiter was deemed "good" and Saturn "bad"—and their effect on other planets reflected this. Jupiter combined with Venus, for example, meant love would increase. Saturn combined with Venus meant love's decrease.

Before continuing, let us first explain what is meant by a planet "combining" with another planet. Let us say that Venus is in the same sign as Jupiter in your chart and they are also in "conjunction"—near one another in longitude. This would be one way they would "combine." We showed this type of aspect on our "clock" in chapter 2.

Another way this conjunction, or combining, can occur would be by transit; that is, your "set" position of Venus in its sign in your birth chart would be affected by Jupiter's "later" position—if that later position coincided with your set Venus by sign and degree proximity. (Remember, *your* Jupiter is also set where it is in your birth chart, in *its* sign, just as your Venus is. In a transit, we are talking about the "moving" Jupiter affecting the set Venus.)

Thus, Venus in conjunction with Jupiter—whether by their natal positions or by transit—would have been designated by astrologers of yore as good, promising love's increase (Venus standing for love), since Jupiter was a benefic. The same thinking would apply to Venus combined with Saturn, who was malefic, thereby boding decrease in love.

Today, most astrologers would characterize Jupiter and Saturn with greater subtlety, avoiding such sharply contrasting terms as *good* and *bad* in favor of more complex and nuanced psychological principles. Although Jupiter will still signify increase, modern astrologers are also aware that there are instances in life when "too much of a good thing" can lead to opposite results. (Consider chocolate! Or any other of our cravings, carried to excess.)

Even something universally good, like love, can often turn out to be a mixed blessing where Jupiter's traditional increase is concerned. From a psychological perspective, Venus and Jupiter combined in a horoscope, for example, can also describe someone who loves too much, who gives everything over to a relationship partner, including her or his personal autonomy. For that person, love's increase comes with a side effect called emotional dependency—and a decrease in self-esteem.

Saturn has the same propensity for restriction in today's astrology as it did in the past. Yet, modern psychology also has shown that adversity or deprivation can actually be spurs to personal achievement for many people. Such individuals are often inspired to work harder in life than others who are more fortunate—to compensate for their initial deficits. As a result, they usually accomplish a great deal and end up feeling good about themselves. Their self-esteem grows, in the face of hardship. For them, what initially appears to be a minus turns out to be a hidden plus.

Saturn's traditional stigma of decrease, or bad fortune, can also bring on a kind of "expect the worst" mentality—even a feeling of paralyzing fear in someone whose chart is being read—until the astrologer applies modern psychological insights. There are times, for example, when we really must confront a bad situation head-on by taking off our rose-colored glasses and looking at something in a more realistic light. This allows us to deal with our difficulty responsibly—and perhaps even to resolve it.

What may have begun as something negative and dreaded can ultimately reward us with great satisfactions and psychological benefits. Similarly, what may have started as something good and happily anticipated can end up disappointing us. In other words, things are not always what they seem. Indeed, they are often the reverse.

Jung called this phenomenon *enantiodromia*. Simply stated, everything sooner or later turns into its opposite. Jung believed this principle governed all aspects of life. Whenever we tend to hold an extreme attitude or position, he stated, a powerful corrective is built up in the psyche. As a result, something inevitably occurs to compensate for our one-sidedness. It is as if we contain some kind of self-regulating mechanism that puts things in psychic balance—not unlike homeostasis in physiology, where a built-in equilibrium is maintained in the body.

In astrology, Jupiter and Saturn demonstrate Jung's principle in their respective symbolisms. Each planet is starkly different in meaning—yet they operate together in the chart in compensatory, corrective ways. When we compare them, they are a study in contrasts. But, as a pair they are woven together to form a single, complementary pattern.

JUPITER AND SATURN AS ASTROLOGICAL PAIRS

Jupiter and Saturn's interrelationship can be seen pictorially in their glyphs: Jupiter's glyph, ♃, depicts the crescent of soul rising above the cross of matter. Symbolically, this says that the soul is paramount with Jupiter, that the soul's quest for fulfillment is the higher way to connect to the material world.

Saturn's glyph, ♄, directly inverts the order: The cross is placed above the crescent. This says that matter is paramount with Saturn, that mastery of the material world is the greater pathway to the soul. Seen as a pair, their glyphs complement each other—each signifying an alternative approach to the integration of soul and matter.

Jupiter stands for the life principle (or archetype) of expansion, of the soul's yearning to grow. It is the principle behind human progress, the impulse to make things better, grander, higher, bigger, greater—in a single word, *more*.

In your horoscope, for example, whatever house Jupiter is placed in is where the verb *to expand* applies. You have self-confidence in that area of life, as well as enthusiasm, exuberance, generosity, largeness of vision, and boundless optimism. Jupiter's planetary disposition is jovial. If we were to personify it, it would be as fat and jolly as Santa Claus—and just as giving.

Jupiter's effects in a chart, however, can be overdone, often needing psychological correction. Generosity in excess can become sheer extravagance, even wastefulness. Self-confidence can also slide into grandiosity. It is then that Saturn—Jupiter's contrasting principle—can come to the rescue with a strong dose of realism, providing the necessary deflation to Jupiter's unlimited expansion. By way of Saturn's counterforce in the horoscope, the astrologer often points the way toward reestablishing psychic balance in a person's life.

In astrology, Saturn stands for the life principle (or archetype) of boundary, summed up in the verb *to restrict*. It is that part of human experience that seeks to contain, limit, consolidate, and define reality. Saturn's rings, as seen in pictures from space, provide an excellent visual metaphor for the planet's symbolic meanings in astrology, as does its position as the outermost planet visible in the sky to the naked eye.

Before the discovery of the invisible planets—Uranus, Neptune, and Pluto—Saturn represented the outer reaches of the universe itself. It was seen as the complete measure of reality, defining the full extent and utmost limit of the human world—its psychic boundary.

The meanings of Saturn in a horoscope include all the relevant terms that apply to boundary: caution, thrift, reserve, and the slow, disciplined building of structure. In your horoscope, therefore, whatever house Saturn is placed in will be where you will put restrictions on things, as you seek to consolidate rather than expand matters. Saturn is serious, taciturn, and dry-humored in its planetary disposition; if we were to personify it, it would be as old and stooped as Father Time—and just as measured.

Saturn's effects in a chart, if overdone, also call out for psychological correction. Caution, if carried to extreme, may be nothing more than a cover-up for inordinate fear, lack of confidence, and stifling inhibition. And what may pass for realism might actually be a substitute for a rigid, self-limiting, and hopelessly pessimistic view of things. It is then that Jupiter can step in, providing a positive antidote to Saturn's gloom and doom. By way of Jupiter's expansive outlook, the astrologer often shows how hope, encouragement, and inspiration can be awakened in a person's life.

Jupiter in astrology also represents faith, not only as hopefulness and positivism but also in a deeply religious sense—as a belief in a benevolent, helpful spiritual power that watches over us like a loving parent. It is the kind of faith evoked in prayers when we ask "our Father who art in heaven" to take care of our wishes and needs, as we would a real father.

Jupiter in Mythology

The name *Jupiter* actually means "God the father," deriving from the Latin term *Diu-pater*. This is surely a fitting description for the divine protector, chief law-giver, spiritual head, and benevolent overseer of Rome—which is who Jupiter *was* in ancient times. He was a benign, caring father figure, which is how he is still seen in his astrological symbolism.

Jupiter's predecessor was Zeus. For the Greeks, Zeus was the king of heaven, a mythic parallel to the brightest, largest planet in the sky. Like Jupiter, he was called the "light-bringer" and was viewed as a luminous presence up above. Zeus was also the bringer of "enlightenment" to mortals below, for his shining light inspired humanity to strive for high ideals. Zeus was said to have invented ethics, for example, giving the concept to humans as a guiding principle so they could live in harmony in cities and in other social groups.

In Jupiter's statuary in Rome, he held the scepter of authority in one hand and the thunderbolt in the other; another emblem of authority, the eagle, was perched on his shoulder. Seated majestically on a throne, Jupiter epitomized divine power. But he also showed the evenhandedness of justice because his thunderbolt could not only demonstrate his wrath but could also bring the gift of rain. As a sky-god, he was called on to replenish the earth in times of drought, as well as imbue society with the light of wisdom in times of conflict and strife.

Jupiter oversaw and inspired Roman law, religious life, and ceremonial rites. He symbolized a kind of spiritual presence that could permeate government, the justice system, and other social institutions, encouraging them to aspire to high principles. His worship embodied a distinct moral conception applicable to all facets of civic life: The code included duty, right dealing, and an allegiance to religion and the state.

In astrology, Jupiter's rulership of Sagittarius—the progressive, fiery sign associated with law, higher learning, ethics, and philosophy, as well as the quest for greater knowledge in service of society—mirrors the god's mythic role as upholder of the social order. Jupiter's connection to faith and religion is also reflected in the planet's corulership of the spiritual sign of Pisces.

In Rome, Jupiter also ruled over the marriage rites. In this regard, he elevated family, domestic life, and the welfare of children into the realm of the sacred. His wife, Juno, presided over childbirth and all traditional female roles. This is also reflected in astrology, where Jupiter is exalted— brought to its highest power—in the protective, maternal, home-oriented sign of Cancer.

The stately Jupiter of the sacred marriage rites was a far cry from the earlier, philandering Zeus of the Greek myths—whose wife, Hera, was famous for throwing jealous fits over her husband's countless infidelities. The unruly, warlike Greek Ares also bears little resemblance to the disciplined, soldierly Mars of Roman times.

All the Greek deities were transformed on the way to the Forum. "When in Rome, do as the Romans do." The gods and goddesses of Greece were given Roman names and dress and absorbed into Roman culture (the Romans had no religious pantheon of their own). And as Rome expanded its imperial power in the centuries around the turn of the millennium, the deities developed, grew, and changed—along with the changing times.

However, the Immortals of Greece carried the same inherent symbolisms in their Roman garb as they had before. Their outer attributes were customized to fit the new regime, but their basic symbolic patterns—their core meanings—remained intact.

Thus, on his way to becoming Jupiter, Zeus's law-giving trait was emphasized, while his famously roving eye was blinkered. Still, he remained the expansive, benevolent, and protective father-god, just as when he reigned in Greece.

In Greek myth, Zeus sired hundreds, maybe thousands of children, fathering gods and goddesses, as well as legendary mortals of epic stature (the famous Helen of Troy, for one). Indeed, his complex interactions with his children are the very stuff of Greek sagas, poems, stories, and myths. In this regard, Zeus was considered, like Jupiter, paterfamilias, the spiritual head of the human family, as well as the patriarch of the Greek people.

Unlike the Romans' Jupiter, however, Zeus is portrayed in many of his stories as a blatant sexual adventurer. He was not above disguising himself in various animal forms, for example, and shamelessly using these ploys to impregnate unsuspecting nymphs. (Helen of Troy herself was born from Leda, who Zeus, in the form of a swan, inseminated.) It is hard to imagine the Roman Jupiter, who shared power with Juno, the guardian and protector of women, exhibiting a similar behavior.

If viewed symbolically, however—which is how myths are best read—

the stories of Zeus's seductions have a more complex and richer meaning. As the god of rain, Zeus had the capacity to seed the earth and make things grow. His stories are metaphors for the life-giving, procreative, generative powers of the universal father. In all his liaisons with nymphs, we have a strong sense of the god's sheer enthusiasm for causing life to multiply, for simply making *more* of it.

Zeus *inspired*, in the word's true meaning, which is to "breathe spirit into"—to make something, or someone, come alive. Nymphs in Greek mythology stood for different features of nature itself: They inhabited woods, meadows, streams, rivers, and mountains, imbuing such places with their qualities, special aura, and mystique.

In espying a nymph, therefore, Zeus saw in her the potential for inspiration, for having her create something new and beautiful, and to be prolific, like nature itself. By assuming an animal shape to accomplish these aims, he also showed how the divine presence is concealed within the instinctual, animalistic force that gives seed to life.

This does not contradict the later Jupiter's inherent meanings, except that they are expressed differently in a Roman setting, to meet the cultural requirements of Roman society and its rather staid, patrician values. The principle of expansion, creation, inspiration, and enthusiasm for growth, as dominant qualities of the good father-god, applies to both Zeus *and* Jupiter.

Jupiter in Astrology

As mirrored in myth, Jupiter in astrology also presents a symbolic image of the father who aspires for his children, who encourages their potential, advances their growth, instills in them confidence, and protects them. He is authority in its most benevolent and supportive aspect.

In your personal horoscope, therefore, Jupiter's placement often shows where the voice of your own good father makes itself heard. It is the voice of inspiration, infusing you with life's creative possibilities and sheer promise. That voice tells you to grow, progress, be confident, cheerful, and optimistic. It encourages you to reach as high as you can and to fulfill your potential—all while keeping an ethical, fair-minded, and societal perspective. It is a voice that says: "Yes, you can. You can do it. Just have faith in yourself. And in the world."

As a kind of meditative exercise, you can imaginatively connect to Jupiter, even without your personal chart in hand. In a quiet space, removed from distractions, simply close your eyes and listen inwardly for your father's voice of encouragement, the voice that speaks the word *yes* to you in any phrasing.

Is there an echo of your actual father's voice in that word? If so, you are one of the lucky ones; you can answer to your real father's voice in your strivings in life. It gives you support and confidence. In your life, your real father is a true inspiration, a guiding light. He affirms your dreams and ideals.

But, if you cannot hear your father's voice, your psychological task, then, is to find the good father in yourself. Listen for Jupiter's voice, however faint it may be at first, for it *is* there, waiting to be heard. Through your own inner work, good friends, support groups, partner, therapist, counselor—or wherever a positive force exists—the good father Jupiter, when sufficiently evoked and sought, will emerge loud and clear in your psyche, and in your life.

With your astrologer you can connect to the powers and strengths of Jupiter in your personal horoscope and make use of these to inspire faith in yourself. Jupiter, the light-bringer, shines within your psyche as it does in the sky, illuminating the path to your own creativity. As a god of myth projected onto the sky, he is but a symbol of your inner light, the light of self-knowledge.

Saturn in Mythology

As a god of myth, Jupiter also had a father. His name was Saturn. We have already spoken of Saturn in astrology as Jupiter's symbolic opposite, as well as his pair. As their family history next unfolds, we see their differences emerge. But we also see how they complement, correct, and balance one another—as only two family members can.

The Greeks knew Saturn as Kronos, one of the first gods to figure in Greek creation-mythology. Kronos was a Titan, a member of a race of giants that ruled the world before there were Olympians, the pantheon of Immortals headed by Zeus. Kronos was not only the father of Zeus but also of Hades, Hestia, Demeter, and Poseidon (in Latin, Pluto, Vesta, Ceres, and Neptune, respectively), as well as of Hera.

Unlike Zeus, however, Kronos did *not* encourage his children to grow. He severely restricted new life, swallowing his newborns before they could develop. He had heard a prophecy that one of his children would usurp his powers; to prevent this, he simply ate each child upon birth. He was a giant but was threatened by the idea that his children would grow larger than him.

Seen symbolically, Kronos is the destructive, devouring father, so different from Zeus, who loved to seed new life, to set his children out into the world and interact dynamically with them. Kronos evokes the image of a father who is so afraid of his children surpassing him that he never allows them to fulfill their life's potential. They do not develop on their own but are kept confined, imprisoned within the controlled borders of Kronos's physical domain.

When it came to the birth of Kronos's last child, Zeus, Kronos's wife Rhea dressed a stone in swaddling clothes and handed it over to her husband, pretending it was the newborn. Keeping to his habit, Kronos swallowed the stone. Meanwhile, Rhea shipped Zeus off to the island of Crete to be secretly raised by nursemaids.

In Crete, Zeus grew into adulthood to fulfill the old prophecy. He took a job as Kronos's cupbearer and slipped a potion into his father's drink; it caused Kronos to regurgitate Zeus's five brothers and sisters, no longer infants but now grown.

Freed from captivity, the disgorged children joined Zeus to battle their father. After a long and brutal struggle, Zeus and his siblings prevailed. Kronos and the other Titans were exiled to the deepest layer of the underworld, a place called Tartarus. The Olympian pantheon was thus begun, with Zeus, their leader, reigning supreme.

Kronos is depicted in pictures and stories holding a sickle. This is because he had earlier supplanted *his* father, Uranus, by castrating him with a sickle (which his mother gave him, since Uranus also unceremoniously disposed of his offspring at birth). We will expand on the story of Uranus—the first father in Greek creation-mythology—in the next chapter.

The Greeks, in their telling of the story, banished Kronos far beneath the underworld; he hardly figures after that in Greek myth. But the Romans resurrected him—sickle and all. He became Saturn, the god of agriculture, and an exalted figure in Roman ceremonial rites, festivals, and religious practices. At harvest time, in particular, the Romans paid their greatest homage to Saturn, since at the reaping of the harvest, it was Saturn's implement, the sickle, that cut down the corn and grain.

The cutting of the corn was a sacred ritual, resonating with death itself. What was planted, grown from a seed, and still green with vitality—

essentially alive—was cut down by Saturn's blade. Such a violent act needed the complicity of a god, and Saturn was worshiped accordingly.

And in yet another way, Saturn also still "ate his children," since he oversaw food: the corn that is also then chewed, swallowed, and devoured. Saturn was also equated by the ancients with time, which "eats up" youth and, like the Grim Reaper's sickle, cuts life short. (The name Kronos itself means time, as in chronology and synchronicity.)

In many depictions of Saturn, he is shown with both the sickle and the hourglass (as old Father Time), as well as a symbol of death (the Grim Reaper). He is also often seen as a crone figure, stooped and withered, but also experienced and wise. In astrology, Saturn encompasses all these meanings—and more.

As a god of the fields and harvest, Saturn stands for hardship, toil, effort, and labor. In astrology, this is reflected in Saturn's rulership of the earthy, industrious sign of Capricorn. As a sign of winter, Capricorn designates a time when the growing season is over. By December, the year is old; its outer look is gray, its heat diminished. The Sun itself seems to be dying.

In the Roman lands, however, this was the time for Saturn's biggest festival, the Saturnalia. At the Saturnalia, the curved arc of Saturn's sickle was transformed into the curved horn of plenty, the cornucopia—a goat's horn (Capricorn being the sign of the goat) overflowing with fruit, flowers, and corn. In the spirit of Jung's principle of "everything turning into its opposite," frugal Saturn now became a god of plenty.

If Saturn's credo is hard work, then the Saturnalia was a time to reap its rewards. People celebrated with wine, dance, and revelry, not only in the countryside but in Rome itself. In the city, banquets, feasts, and parties were held in honor of the god.

Saturn now represented abundance, overflowing wealth, joy, and pleasure. He was no longer inhibited; toast after toast were made to him by inebriated, ecstatic worshipers—Roman matrons and soldiers alike. Indeed, the rigid social barriers of Roman life came down at the Saturnalia, when Saturn's traditional boundaries no longer held. There is an echo of this in astrology, with Saturn's corulership of Aquarius, the zodiac's egalitarian, "rule-breaking" sign.

In similar fashion, Saturn's principle of restriction is a paradox. As a symbol of work, he both limits us and feeds us: He deprives us of time yet provides a reward. In astrology, Saturn is often called the teacher. If we do the homework, we get the *A*. Accordingly, every achievement in life extracts its price: What you put in, you get back in kind. This credo is reflected in Saturn's exaltation in Libra, the sign of fairness and balance.

Saturn in Astrology

As a symbolic planetary figure, Saturn is complex and multifaceted (as are all the planets in astrology). When we regard Saturn as the devouring father, there is a distinctly negative cast to him. For example, in a chart a tyrannical, authoritarian, or oppressive father often shows up by way of Saturn. Like Kronos of old, this father is one whose voice says "no," who cuts off our potential, limits our growth, and keeps us confined within the rigid rings of his controlled, airless, and claustrophobic universe.

We are also devoured by Saturn when we are eaten away by worry, self-doubt, fear, and insecurity. In alchemy, Saturn was associated with lead, which represents all things heavy, cold, rigid, and hardened. His name was also linked with the black bile of melancholia—what today we call depression.

In a less extreme—and more typical way—Saturn in the horoscope is the father's voice of experience, which can resound with your real father's voice if he served as your mentor. Or you can call on your own inner voice of authority, which you can summon by finding the place of practical wisdom within yourself. It says: "Prepare the groundwork for what you want in life. And build upon it, piece by piece. Do your work, but do not raise your hopes too high. Nothing comes easily."

In the Hindu epic, the *Mahabharata*, a short parable succinctly sums up Saturn's meaning in astrology. It reads as follows:

> The peasant tends the earth with his plough, next he sows, then he waits, arms folded. The crop will come from the clouds. If the rains don't fall, he won't blame himself, he will say, "I worked like the others, the rain did not come, it's not my fault." But if he hadn't worked, if he hadn't sown, what fruit could he expect?

Jupiter, in his symbolism, promises the rain. It may or may not come. He is the god of faith, hope, and charity. We look to him in the swollen clouds of blue heaven; he is cloud nine.

Saturn, in his symbolism, simply hands us the sickle—placing the responsibility on us to work our plot.

uranus, neptune, and pluto:

Avatars of Change

URANUS, DIVINE AWAKENER

On March 13, 1781, an amateur astronomer named William Herschel set up a homemade telescope in his backyard garden in Bath, England. Between 10 P.M. and 11 P.M., his lenses picked up an uncommonly large, brightly glowing disk of light, which he initially thought was an unknown star or comet. But what Herschel had sighted was a new planet—Uranus—the first beyond Saturn in our solar system.

This was a cataclysmic discovery. The ancient, time-honored universe suddenly expanded to twice its size, and Saturn no longer defined its outer reaches. And with Saturn's age-old boundary shattered, the world of outer space was never the same. It was as if heaven itself had split wide open, showing the way to a new, far-flung idea of itself.

A new social concept also emerged during Herschel's time, breaking down old, rigid, and limiting structures. It went by many names: liberty, freedom, the revolt against the established order, the end of tyrannical authority. In a single word, its name was revolution.

The American Revolution, of 1776, was soon followed by the French Revolution—with such innovative ideas as human progress, equality, and individual rights suddenly erupting from the mind of the people. The new machines of the industrial revolution were already rolling along at full force, toppling old class systems along with outmoded ways of thinking.

Uranus's discovery coincided with a historical age when breakthroughs in science and technology were happening at rapid speed. A spate of new inventions forever changed the way people lived, worked, and related to one another, not only in Europe and America but worldwide. This was the Age of Enlightenment, when new ideas surged through the globe like electricity—which was also developed during this period by such pioneers as Galvani, Ben Franklin, Volta, Ampere, and Ohm.

In astrology, the planet Uranus conjures up the electrifying spirit of its time of discovery. It is a spirit of revolution, rebellion, independence, new directions, inventions, and startling, unpredictable occurrences. Reflecting all this, Uranus signifies that place in the horoscope—and in our lives—where things abruptly change their course and take a sudden turn, for better or for worse. It is also where an old, habitual structure is broken. As a result, things are never the same.

Thus, Uranus's psychological effect can often be disruptive and volatile—even violent—leaving instability in its wake. We are shaken, shocked, and disoriented because of it. But the effects can also be liberating, since they force us to deal with life events, people, ourselves, and our current situation from a fresh perspective. The very suddenness of Uranus's impact on us acts as a kind of wake-up call, making us see things in a new and more conscious way.

In this sense, Uranus in astrology is often called the Awakener, because the planet's effects in the horoscope cause us to become aware of things in an acute, immediate, direct, and sudden way. We are typically in "Saturn's world" before a Uranus-type upheaval, which is usually brought on by a transit—a later position of Uranus impacting on a set position of a planet in the birth chart. Saturn's world is one of predictability, order, structure, and well-defined boundary. However, on some other level of our being, we also feel profoundly bored, unstimulated, and stagnant. Then, like a bolt out of the blue, something happens—internally, externally, or both—to force a change.

We suddenly lose a job, for example. Or we are stunned by a revelation in our marriage, family, friendship, business relationship, or in any number of life situations. We may have an accident or some kind of emotional set-back. Or we may experience a major financial loss—or a sudden windfall. Or something may occur of a shocking, disruptive, and unexpected nature— good or bad—that irrevocably changes the map of our everyday life.

A Uranus transit can also be a time when we are inexplicably impulsive, feeling restless, reckless, or both. Others might say we are acting "out of character." This is a time when we quit a job, for example, or walk out on a marriage, startle friends, upset the apple cart, or cause a mishap.

However, after the initial dislocation, we often find that a gate has sud-denly been opened on a new vista of life. We feel invigorated, liberated, psychologically freed—and are now able to progress to a heightened level of experience that had somehow been unavailable to us before Uranus's revolutionary impact.

Thus, in the horoscope Uranus acts as a kind of psychic alarm clock, abruptly waking us. It has us open our eyes all at once, letting us know that we had been asleep too long. In its symbolism in the chart, Uranus is about our awakening from slumber into a conscious state of being; it represents the mind when it is keenly aware of situations.

Uranus is also known in astrology as the planet of the "higher mind," a kind of impersonal world soul that transcends humanity but is also energetically connected to it. Its glyph, ♅, pictorially captures this idea of a world soul, the fact of *two* crescents on either side of the cross emphasizing the predominance of soul overseeing the material world.

According to astrologer Alan Oken in *As Above, So Below*, one crescent signifies the collective soul, the other the individual soul. They are linked together on the Earth plane (the cross of matter). Suspended from the cross is a small circle, which represents the vitalizing spirit underlying all matter.

On a more whimsical note, Alice Howell, in her book *Jungian Symbolism in Astrology*, describes Uranus's glyph as the ubiquitous rooftop television antenna. She states: "The process of Uranus has to do with invisible energy and its transmission. It is the higher octave of Mercury and works at another level of communication, an almost instantaneous one."

Uranus's connection to the higher mind is also seen in its rulership of the airy, intellectual, abstract, and mentally detached sign of Aquarius. The Aquarian idealism—its altruism, progressive thinking, and humanitarian, one-world outlook—also coincides with Uranus's astrological meanings.

In Greek myth, Uranus symbolized the divine higher mind that invented the world. He was said to have designed the wings of the butterfly, for example. (Interestingly, the Greek name for butterfly is *psyche*, the same word for soul.) Uranus was the original Greek sky-god of creation. He awakened Mother Nature, whose name was Gaia, with his thunderbolt and lightning, impregnating her with the fertilizing seed of rain. In doing so, he awakened life itself because, as the first father of Greek story, he set off the chain of events that led to life's unfolding.

But Uranus found his progeny with Gaia ugly. They were the giant Titans, assorted monsters, and also the Cyclopes, one-eyed creatures of colossal proportion. They did not match his ideal: perfection. So he buried his children one by one, pushing them back into the womb of Mother Earth.

This imagery symbolically portrays the father who has a preconceived, idealized notion of how his children should turn out. But his children are never good enough to meet his standards or high expectations. They disappoint him, so he pushes them down, often into the mother's more protective, all-embracing realm.

In astrology, the Uranus myth is often used to explore such psychological issues. When they reveal themselves in the chart through the planet Uranus, the father is often the "genius" or iconoclast, the highly accomplished, inventive sort, a kind of unapproachable sky-figure, one whose ideals are impossible for his children to live up to.

However, whatever is pushed down inevitably erupts, rebels, or turns monstrous. As we have seen in the previous chapter, in the story, Gaia could no longer bear the burden, so she handed the last-born child, Kronos, the sickle. He used it to castrate his father. From the blood that dripped to the ground, the Furies were born, spawning hatred, violence, and rage in the world. Yet, when Kronos then cast his father's genitals into the sea, love also emerged from its depths—in the form of Aphrodite, born of the sea foam.

In the myth, then, the opposites of hate and love were equally created by Uranus's cast-off seed. Also in the myth, it is Saturn, the limiter, who breaks free from the repressive binds of Uranus (only to repeat his father's pattern). It appears from his myth that the world Uranus generated is full of contrast, discrepancy, and paradox.

These very incongruities perfectly capture the contradictory spirit of Uranus in astrology. Its planetary nature is highly rational yet maddeningly irrational. It symbolizes the logical, cerebral, and scientific mind, yet it also brings on wild, inconsistent, even chaotic thinking. Its outlook is collective and humanitarian, yet it stresses independent and individual action.

Uranus is simply a planet of inconsistencies. Its energies are erratic, deviant, quirky, unusual—and often perverse. As if to underscore this, the actual planet is tilted almost 100 degrees on its axis, seeming to spin sideways.

In horoscope interpretation, Uranus's eccentric nature invariably causes even the most predictive of astrologers to refrain from uttering a single prediction—except, perhaps, to say, "Expect the unexpected!" Because, like life itself, Uranus, the divine awakener, is full of surprises.

NEPTUNE, DIVINE DREAMER

Before its actual discovery, the planet Neptune was only a figment of scientific imagination. It was *believed* to exist because some unseen celestial force seemed to be influencing Uranus's orbit, causing it to vary in irregular ways, called "perturbations." Thus, Neptune began as a hypothetical entity, an allusion, before it was actually sighted via telescope by German astronomer Johann Galle, on September 23, 1846.

In history, Neptune's discovery came at the peak of Romanticism, a movement that swept over Europe and Russia as a kind of counterreaction to the Enlightenment's emphasis on reason, empirical science, and technology. Romanticism, in contrast, was anti-intellectual, primarily seeking to appeal to people's hearts and souls—by way of their emotions.

To its adherents, such things as feelings, impressions, moods, soulful yearnings, and intuition had more value than the purely conceptual power of the mind. Romanticism also explored spiritual themes, as well as the power of imagination and creative inspiration in life.

Romanticism was expressed most vividly in art, music, literature, and dance—but its effects were also evident in the day's social and political movements. The exalted, if unrealistic, aspirations for humanity that influenced such nineteenth-century ideas as socialism, utopianism, and communism reflected an underlying romantic, glorified vision of the world. It was a vision based on classless societies, with shared wealth, mutual sacrifice, cooperation, and community.

As with Uranus, Neptune's astrological meanings are captured by the spirit of the time of its discovery. It is a spirit contained in the word *romantic* itself—a word that conjures up a deeply felt emotional longing. Illusion, fantasy, wistfulness, and reverie also belong to the symbolic realm of Neptune in astrology.

Neptune's invisible influence from afar, as well as its imaginary status before its discovery, also resonate with the planet's meanings in astrology. Its subtle yet powerful effects in the horoscope enhance our capacity to imagine, envision, and intuit things, putting us in touch with a kind of unseen, subliminal, mysterious world.

Neptune signifies a place in the horoscope—and in our lives—where we *believe*, where we have an all-embracing trust in something intangible yet unmistakably true for us. We feel, sense, or have a premonition of something we know as real without our being able to explain it rationally. As a personified figure embodying these descriptives, Neptune stands for the seer, prophet, psychic, or mystic in each of us.

Dreams, wishes, illusory images, fantasies, and the like—along with their creative by-products in art, film, photography, and other expressive fields—involve Neptune in astrology. As a matter of fact, the first photograph, taken with a device called a camera obscura (*obscure* is a key Neptune word in astrology), was created at the time of Neptune's discovery, as was the daguerreotype, an early type of photograph.

In its most positive sense, Neptune in astrology signifies the elevation of spiritual values. In its symbolism, the planet represents a part of us that is creative, imaginative, psychic, and poetic. Its influence in the horoscope connects us to our internal life and its rich, soulful imagery. Neptune honors not only the mystic in each of us but also the artist.

Neptune's influence in the horoscope draws us deeply into ourselves, supporting our psychological need for solitude, contemplation, inner peace, and serenity. Under its effects, we long to escape from everyday reality—and tend to do so. At such times, we may find ourselves immersed in a sea of inner images—in particular, the elusive images of dreams because Neptune lulls us into the world of sleep. In sleep, when consciousness dissolves, we are pulled into Neptune's half-lit, vague, fleeting, and amorphous realm.

As in sleep and dreams, Neptune's effects in the horoscope can make us feel as if things are blurred, undefined, and seeping into other things. We become unmoored, so to speak, as we slowly drift from matters that had previously engaged us. We are distracted, unclear in our goals, and utterly confused. We feel as if things are slipping away from us.

In its negative sense, when Neptune has its psychological hold on us, we passively "go with the flow," floating along aimlessly in life. We also tend to cling emotionally, or spiritually, to another person, group, cause, or any other "anchor" in our line of sight, meanwhile giving ourselves over—because, with Neptune's dissolving powers, our sense of personal identity is lost. This effect of Neptune can often open us to emotional abuse and victimhood.

The imagery of the sea, with all its metaphors, is also conjured up by Neptune in astrology. The sea provides a vision of boundlessness, sheer beauty, and fathomless depth, perfectly capturing Neptune's romantic aura. To look out at its wide expanse or sail on its waters can be calming, restorative, and profoundly healing to the soul. But we can also become lost in its vastness, be submerged, and drown in its undertow.

In this last sense, Neptune's escapist tendencies often result in a bottomless plunge into alcoholism, or lead to dependencies on opiates, psychedelics, mood- and mind-altering drugs, tranquilizers, or any other type of intoxicant that blurs reality, or helps us escape consciously dealing with it.

Issues of alcohol and drug addiction are typically explored by way of Neptune in astrology. However, such issues are also often seen by many astrologers as the soul's misdirected longings for transcendence and ecstasy—a kind of misguided religious yearning. The great success of twelve-step recovery programs, with their underlying spiritual message, attests to the practical validity of this type of approach.

According to its placement in the astrological chart, Neptune also often shows us where family structures, roles, and boundaries are blurred or dissolved. In such cases, the planet is the signifier of an alcoholic, missing, weak, or absent parent—or of a victimized, or emotionally abused father or mother.

In a more positive sense, the parent signified by Neptune may simply be perceived as artistic or otherwise creative—or merely spacey, dreamy, or reclusive. Planets in astrology carry a full range of meaning within their dominant symbolism. When working directly with the person in question, it is always the astrologer's task to extract more specific contents, as well as their psychological effects.

In mythology, Neptune was the Roman god of the sea, known as Poseidon to the Greeks. His brother Zeus gave him the underwater realm to rule after the victorious war with the Titans. Neptune's astrological glyph, ♆, is a pictograph of the trident, the three-pronged spear always held by the bearded sea-god, even in modern representations.

As an astrological symbol, the glyph depicts the crescent of soul pierced by the cross of matter, suggesting the interpenetration of soul and matter as part of Neptune's meaning. The trident is also a stylized version of the implement actually used for spearing fish, amplifying Neptune's rulership in astrology of watery, elusive Pisces, the sign of the fish. Like the fish, and water itself, Neptune's effects in the horoscope are often difficult to fully grasp or hold on to. They are subtle, ambiguous, nebulous, nuanced, and deceptive.

When Neptune is affecting our chart (usually by way of a transit, a later position of Neptune impacting on a set position of a planet in the birth chart), the planet's influence is slow, unclear, and gradual—yet deeply transformative. We have a vague impression that something is being sacrificed in our lives. We have renounced some previous attachment, not in a sudden, shocking, or unexpected way, as with Uranus, but in an almost imperceptible way. It simply disintegrates, drifts away, or fogs up with uncertainty.

With the impact of Uranus, for example, we might be fired from a job without warning. With Neptune, however, it is more likely that the job itself would disappear—it might be shifted to another department, for example—in a process that may have been going on for a while but was not apparent to us. We eventually let go, or realize it is time to leave, but it happens in a gradual, unobtrusive way.

Similarly, in a relationship, when Neptune permeates the horoscope there is no sudden breakup, or flare-up, or unexpected development, as with Uranus. Instead, there is a kind of slow erosion of love, a drifting apart that goes unnoticed—until it simply dissolves. The impact on us is profound, but its blow is subdued, muted, even gentle.

Neptune is described in astrology as a higher octave of Venus, since its vibratory energies elicit a more exalted form of love than Venus's often purely physical expressions. The typical kinds of relatedness that Venus evokes in the chart are transformed by Neptune into spiritual love—agape—expressed as compassion, kindness, sympathy, and selfless service. In this sense, Neptune also personifies the figure of the saint, or the savior. If carried too far, however, the saint or savior can turn into the martyr.

Neptune casts a veil over everything it touches in the horoscope. The Hindus characterize such a veil as *maya*, the Sanskrit word for illusion. *Maya* is also the word for the origin of life itself, traditionally symbolized in myth as the primordial waters of the sea, Neptune's realm.

If we translate Neptune's watery realm into psychological terms, we discover the planet's meaning in astrology to be the great, fathomless sea of the unconscious itself—with its rich store of sunken treasures, hidden caves, and fleeting forms that are "such stuff as dreams are made on." In a word, it is *maya*.

PLUTO, DIVINE DESTROYER

At the outer reaches of our solar system, at its farthest point, is Pluto, a small, icy planet, shrouded in semidarkness. It faces the dim, distant light of the Sun from across an enormous chasm of bleak, empty space. Isolated from the family of planets clustered near the Sun, its closest neighbor, Neptune, is one billion miles away. Facing away from the Sun, Pluto looks out onto the very edge of darkness—an immense void extending toward the innumerable worlds beyond.

For us here on Earth, basking in the bright, golden Sun, dimly lit Pluto seems dark, enigmatic, and inconceivably far away. The vast distance between us, combined with the planet's relatively small size, renders Pluto utterly invisible to the naked eye. Even with the aid of high-powered modern telescopes, it is difficult to discern.

Indeed, Pluto was only fairly recently brought to light with its discovery on February 18, 1930. Decades before it was actually sighted, however, noted astronomer Percival Lowell was convinced of the planet's existence and began to search for it. He knew that Uranus's perturbations could not be fully explained, even after the discovery of Neptune. Lowell actually died before Pluto was finally pinpointed by another astronomer, Clyde Tombaugh (by way of a special device called a blink telescope), but it is Lowell who is credited for laying the scientific groundwork for its discovery. (Strangely, the perturbations of Uranus are still not fully accounted for!)

Pluto's astrological glyph, ♇, depicts Percival Lowell's initials, as well as the first two letters of the planet's name. The alternative astrological glyph for Pluto, ♀, synthesizes the symbolic meanings of the circle of spirit, the crescent of soul, and the cross of matter. Spirit is here contained by soul, as if floating within it. Together, from above, they powerfully combine to permeate the physical world below.

Pluto's meanings in the horoscope are captured by the metaphor of its solitary placement in outer space, evoking imagery of alienation, isolation, and separation. Its psychological effects resonate with our archaic fear of the dark, causing profound feelings of dread, along with a frightening anticipation of unknown, unseen, shadowy worlds beyond our own. In this last sense, Pluto in astrology conjures up the idea of the fearful end— of death itself.

As Saturn was in the ancient world, Pluto in the modern world is poised at the outer edge of our solar system. There are many differences, however, in how Saturn and Pluto are described in astrology, and in the meanings they evoke in the horoscope—despite each planet's association with death.

The universe of Saturn's time was envisioned as a closed system, while the modern universe is perceived as expanding and infinite, existing beyond the confines of ordinary space and time. The planet Saturn, visible to the naked eye, literally defined the outer boundary of the ancient world. As such, it was the end-all and be-all of material, time-bound earthly existence.

Saturn's influence in the horoscope, correspondingly, is limited to a manageable sphere of action within the real world. On a symbolic level, the planet's finality in the solar system was seen to mirror life's finite nature— which, in turn, was reflected in agriculture and its reliance on time-bound cycles and seasons. With Saturn, death was part of the process of time and physicality.

However, in a timeless, expanding universe, Pluto's position at the brink of our solar system evokes the imagery of a planet that goes "beyond" death, one that symbolically stands at the invisible border between one cosmic sphere and another. Pluto evokes an idea of death as transformation, not as finality. This is the essential meaning of Pluto in the astrological chart: While it is the planet symbolizing death, it is more about the process of transformation from one psychic state to another.

Pluto was discovered when the world itself was beginning to experience its precarious existence. Humankind could suddenly imagine the prospect of its total death—since Pluto was discovered on the verge of the Atomic Age. Plutonium, named for Pluto, was first made (by nuclear fission) during this period, an era that also saw the unleashing of other dangerous and destructive forces in the world. Despair, already brought on by the Great Depression, had also cast its dark cloud over everything. Like Pluto, the world stood at the edge of an abyss in the 1930s, facing into darkness.

In keeping with the alienating spirit of its time of discovery, Pluto's effects in the horoscope elicit similar feelings of despair, along with a profound sense of danger, even annihilation. When the planet is activated in the chart (usually by way of a transit, a later position of Pluto impacting on a set position of a planet in the birth chart), we experience something powerful, something completely beyond our control—as if an inexorable force is rolling over our lives, wreaking emotional havoc. And, as with the other outer planets, Uranus and Neptune, things are never the same.

As the planet of transformation, Pluto in astrology symbolizes the concept of regeneration, a kind of psychic rebirth that can occur after sheer destruction. Like Scorpio, the powerful, resourceful sign it rules, Pluto also extracts from us our hidden strengths for the purpose of psychological recovery. Scorpio's visual imagery of the phoenix rising from the ashes of destruction also applies to its ruling planet.

Pluto's effects in the horoscope, therefore, are twofold: With Pluto, an old mode of being is irrevocably destroyed, but we are also compelled, psychologically, to create something new. The very power of the emotional experience of death—whether of a person, relationship, or anything of importance in our lives—somehow fuels the change and gives us the necessary strength to regenerate.

At such times, we are called on, psychologically, to reinvent ourselves, to shed an old skin and begin anew. The call to change may occur spontaneously, from some deep, inner stirring, or by way of an outer event. In either case, we feel that something must shift drastically, both inwardly and outwardly—or we will "die" in some profound emotional way.

Pluto's impact on the horoscope may signal the end of a relationship, for example, but it also brings to the surface complicated psychological issues—for example, a sexual triangle, money scheme, festering grievance, or secret obsession—that force us to change radically. In simpler scenarios, Pluto's impact may cause us to get rid of our possessions, drop old friends, shed pounds, sell our home, move, or radically change our lifestyle. By putting an end to an old self, our new self is rejuvenated.

In myth, Pluto was the Roman name for the Greek god Pluton, whom the Greeks also knew as Hades. He was the god of the dead, and, as such, he ruled over the dark, gloomy, barren realm that was envisioned by the ancients as being beneath the earth. Pluto had dominion over all the departed souls that dwelled within his depths; he opened the gates of the earth when they descended. Symbolically, to enter his realm meant going down into a deeper level of reality.

On a few occasions, Pluto would ascend to the upper world to capture a desired soul. He donned a special helmet that rendered him invisible, and—like death itself—took someone down to his depths, unseen. This is an apt metaphor for Pluto's powerful influence in the astrological chart because we are always "taken down" by Pluto to that deeper level of reality—one way or the other.

In the most extreme of examples, we may find ourselves in the shadowy world of drugs, violence, or crime. Or we may be a party to some Faustian scheme that holds us in its grip. Or we are caught in a dire emotional situation: sexual trauma, incest, or rape. In less drastic, and more common instances, we are simply led down into darker areas of our own psychology, parts that previously may have been unseen by us—perhaps by way of psychoanalysis or by other probings of our psychic depths.

Pluto's kingdom beneath the earth paralleled that of his brother Neptune, who ruled beneath the sea. Symbolically, each reigned over an invisible, deep, dimly perceived yet powerful sphere of existence. When Zeus divided up the spoils of victory over the Titans, he took the upper world—the realm of the sky, and the bright light of consciousness it represented. As god of thunder, lightning, and rain, he could influence humanity from above, dispensing his gifts from high on Mount Olympus. To his two brothers, he relegated what was left.

In modern psychological terms, what Zeus, the light-bringer, actually consigned to his brothers was the concealed, murky underworld realm of the psyche—the part not "needed" by consciousness. We have already explored Neptune's submerged, underwater domain, where amorphous, fluid, dreamlike imagery is contained.

Pluto's domain of the psyche can be characterized in Freudian psychology as the subconscious, where unacceptable (to the conscious ego) feelings, ideas, emotions, wishes, fantasies, attitudes, and opinions are repressed. Freud also spoke of the id, which exists on a deeper level of the subconscious—where primitive drives, impulses, and instincts (such as sex, hunger, and aggression) are implacably rooted.

In astrology, Pluto's meanings embrace the full emotional range of the Freudian subconscious, including the id. Typically, issues such as jealousies, hatreds, rages, obsessions, compulsions, infantile desires, fixations, and other hidden complexes of the personality are explored by way of Pluto in the horoscope. Sexual themes are also included in Pluto's domain— spanning everything from matters of emotional intimacy to the more deeply embedded and damaging experiences of sexual abuse.

Jung's term for the underworld space symbolized by Pluto is the "personal unconscious." It is the psychic home of what Jung called the "shadow," or shadow-side of the conscious personality, housing those aspects we wish to conceal, deny, disown, or repress. Like Freud's subconscious, the personal unconscious is also a place where we keep our demons.

But for Jung our demons are there to "compensate" for our angels, so that they serve as a kind of psychic corrective to a one-sided conscious attitude. In other words, they are there for a purpose, which is to unify the personality and recognize its wholeness. Or, as the poet Rainer Rilke so eloquently wrote: "If my devils are to leave me, I am afraid my angels will take flight as well."

From the Jungian perspective, if the "upper" personality is demonic, the shadow-side will contain something good, a hidden nugget of psychological gold, so to speak. It suggests that a kind of angel dwells in even the worst of us, if only we knew how to free it from its underground dungeon.

Jung believed that the shadow is a kind of treasure, a hidden resource that can ultimately be mined for psychological healing. This coincides with Pluto's mythological meanings, since Pluto was also known to the ancients as the god of invisible riches, the keeper of the wealth concealed beneath the earth. Similarly, the astrological Pluto compels us to dig deeply into our psychic darkness so that we may bring to the surface the hidden world of riches buried deep within us.

CONCLUSION

The planets of astrology are the gods and goddesses within us. Their conflicts, rises and falls, roles, relationships, losses, loves, and sorrows are the same as ours. Their stories are the stories of the whole human family. They are also the stories of a single psychic domain—yours. You contain the bright, glowing light of the Sun, as well as varying shades of darkness. Each planet dwells in your firmament.

In this same spirit, astrology—by way of all the planets interacting in the horoscope—attempts to mine the whole person, to explore his or her wholeness. The chart we are born with is unfinished, as we are. It is our task—indeed, our life's work—to fulfill it. Not to perfect it, because it is already perfect, but to complete it.

This means we must suffer our contradictions, grapple with their differences, and hold their opposing forces at bay—yet somehow find the wisdom to unite them. This is the essence of the astrological work.

Resources

ASTROLOGICAL CHART SERVICES

The following three major firms offer astrological chart services for a modest fee. You must provide your birth data. In return you will receive a computer-generated personal horoscope. When ordering, have the following information ready for each horoscope requested:

> date of birth
> time of birth
> place of birth

These firms offer a variety of astrological services, such as compatibility charts; relocation charts; natal profile reports; yearly, monthly, or daily planetary guides; and all manner of chart wheels. Send or call for more information.

Astro Communications Services, Inc.
5521 Ruffin Road
San Diego, California 92123
1-800-888-9983
(619) 492-9919
http://www.astrocom.com

Astrolabe
P.O. Box 1750
Brewster, Massachusetts 02631
1-800-843-6682
(508) 896-5081
http://www.alabe.com

Astrology Center of America
P.O. Box 10170
Santa Fe, New Mexico 87504
1-800-475-2272
(505) 989-1857
Fax (505) 989-1858
http://www.astroamerica.com/index.html

WEBSITES

At the following websites, your personal horoscope will be calculated online free of charge. Your birth information must be entered, as stated above.

Astrodienst
http://www.astro.ch/atlas

Astrolabe
http://www.alabe.com

Astrolog 5.30 freeware
http://www.magitech.com/~cruiser1/astrolog/htm

The following websites provide excellent astrological information online and a wide variety of resources:

>Matrix
>http://205.186.189.2/astrology/astrology.htm
>
>Metalog
>http://www.astrologer.com
>
>Zodiacal Zephyr
>http://www.zodiacal.com

VITAL RECORDS

To obtain a copy of your birth certificate, write, visit, or call your local office of vital statistics. *Always specify that you request the long form containing the time of birth.*

For a very nominal fee, you can also order the U.S. government publication, *Where to Write for Vital Records*, published by the U.S. Department of Health and Human Services, from:

>Superintendent of Documents
>U.S. Government Printing Office
>Washington, DC 20402

Ask for the *latest* issue of the above title, DDHS Publication No. (PHS) 1142

This handy booklet lists all the offices of vital records in all fifty states, plus American Samoa, the Canal Zone, the District of Columbia, Guam, the Mariana Islands, Puerto Rico, Saipon, and the Virgin Islands.

NATIONAL ORGANIZATIONS

For information on accredited astrologers and teachers, as well as astrological lectures, classes, and conferences in your area, contact these national organizations:

American Federation of Astrologers, Inc. (AFA)
P.O. Box 22040
6535 South Rural Road
Tempe, Arizona 85285
(602) 838-1751
http://www.astrologers.com

National Council for Geocosmic Research, Inc. (NCGR)
9307 Thornewood Drive
Baltimore, Maryland 21234
(410) 665-6222
http://www.geocosmic.org

ʙiblioɡɾɑpʜy

INTRODUCTION

Barz, Ellynor. *Gods and Planets: The Archetypes of Astrology*. Wilmette, Ill.: Chiron Publications, 1993.

Edinger, Edward F. *The Eternal Drama: The Inner Meaning of Greek Mythology*. Boston and London: Shambhala, 1994.

Guttman, Ariel, and Kenneth Johnson. *Mythic Astrology: Archetypal Powers in the Horoscope*. St. Paul, Minn.: Llewellyn Publications, 1993.

Jung, Carl G. "On the Nature of the Psyche." In *The Structure and Dynamics of the Psyche*. Volume 8 of the *Collected Works of C. G. Jung*. Princeton, N.J.: Princeton University Press, 1969.

Samuels, Andrew, Bani Shorter, and Fred Plaut. *A Critical Dictionary of Jungian Analysis*. London and New York: Routledge, 1986.

CHAPTER 1

Aveni, Anthony. *Behind the Crystal Ball: Magic & Science from Antiquity Through the New Age*. New York: Random House, 1996.

———. *Conversing with the Planets: How Science & Myth Invented the Cosmos*. New York and Tokyo: Kodansha, 1994.

Bless, R. C. *Discovering the Cosmos*. Sausalito, Calif.: University Science Books, 1996.

Freud, Sigmund. "The Unconscious." In *Collected Papers of Sigmund Freud, Volume IV*. New York: Basic Books, Inc., 1959.

Howell, Alice O. *Jungian Synchronicity in Astrological Signs and Ages*. Wheaton, Ill.: Quest Books, 1990.

Jobes, Gertrude, and James Jobes. *Outer Space: Myths, Name Meanings, Calendars*. New York and London: The Scarecrow Press, Inc., 1964.

Jung, Carl G. "The Psychology of the Transference." In *The Practice of Psychotherapy*. Volume 16 of the *Collected Works of C. G. Jung*. Princeton, N.J.: Princeton University Press, 1966.

Krupp, E. C. *Beyond the Blue Horizon: Myths & Legends of the Sun, Moon, Stars & Planets*. New York: HarperCollins, 1991.

Pannekoek, A. *A History of Astronomy*. New York: Dover Publications, Inc., 1989.

Pritchard, J. B. *Ancient Near Eastern Texts Relating to the Old Testament*. Princeton, N.J.: Princeton University Press, 1983.

Tester, Jim. *A History of Western Astrology*. New York: Ballantine Books, 1989.

Thompson, R. Campbell. *The Reports of the Magicians and Astrologers of Ninevah and Babylon in the British Museum*. London: Luza and Company, 1900.

CHAPTER 2

Aveni, Anthony. *Behind the Crystal Ball: Magic & Science from Antiquity Through the New Age*. New York: Random House, 1996.

———. *Conversing with the Planets: How Science & Myth Invented the Cosmos*. New York and Tokyo: Kodansha, 1994.

———. *Empires of Time: Calendars, Clocks, and Cultures*. New York and Tokyo: Kodansha, 1995.

deVore, Nicholas. *Encyclopedia of Astrology*. New York: Philosophical Library, 1947.

Dreyer, Ronnie Gale. *Vedic Astrology: A Guide to the Fundamentals of Jyotish.* York Beach, Maine: Samuel Weiser, Inc., 1997.

Gettings, Fred. *The Arkana Dictionary of Astrology*, rev. ed. New York and London: Penguin, 1990.

Henderson, John S. *The World of the Ancient Maya*, 2d edition. Ithaca, N.Y.: Cornell University Press, 1997.

Jobes, Gertrude, and James Jobes. *Outer Space: Myths, Name Meanings, Calendars.* New York and London: The Scarecrow Press, Inc., 1964.

Kwok, Man-Ho. *Chinese Astrology.* Boston: Tuttle Publishers, 1997.

Lau, Theodora. *The Handbook of Chinese Horoscopes*, rev. ed. New York: Harper and Row, 1988.

Oken, Alan. "Hindu Joytisha-Shastra: The Art of Hindu Astrology." In *Astrology: Evolution & Revolution.* New York: Bantam Books, 1976.

Pannekoek, A. *A History of Astronomy.* New York: Dover Publications, Inc., 1989.

Tester, Jim. *A History of Western Astrology.* New York: Ballantine Books, 1989.

CHAPTER 3

Aveni, Anthony. *Conversing with the Planets: How Science & Myth Invented the Cosmos.* New York and Tokyo: Kodansha, 1994.

Degani, Meir H. *Astronomy Made Simple.* Garden City, N.Y.: Doubleday and Company, Inc., 1976.

deVore, Nicholas. *Encyclopedia of Astrology.* New York: Philosophical Library, 1947.

Dreyer, Ronnie Gale. *Vedic Astrology: A Guide to the Fundamentals of Jyotish.* York Beach, Maine: Samuel Weiser, Inc., 1997.

Gettings, Fred. *The Arkana Dictionary of Astrology*, rev. ed. New York and London: Penguin, 1990.

Hand, Robert. *Horoscope Symbols.* West Chester, Penn.: Whitford Press, 1981.

Hone, Margaret E. *The Modern Text-Book of Astrology.* Essex, England: L.N. Fowler and Co. Ltd., 1978.

March, Marion D., and Joan McEvers. *The Only Way to . . . Learn Astrology: Basic Principles, Volume I.* San Diego: ACS Publications, Inc., 1981.

Mayo, Jeff. *Teach Yourself Astrology.* Kent, England: Hodder and Stoughton Ltd., 1979.

Oken, Alan. *As Above, So Below.* New York: Bantam Books, 1973.

Tester, Jim. *A History of Western Astrology.* New York: Ballantine Books, 1989.

CHAPTER 4

Greene, Liz. *The Astrology of Fate*. York Beach, Maine: Samuel Weiser, Inc., 1984.

Guttman, Ariel, and Kenneth Johnson. *Mythic Astrology: Archetypal Powers in the Horoscope*. St. Paul, Minn.: Llewellyn Publications, 1993.

Howell, Alice O. *Jungian Symbolism in Astrology*. Wheaton, Ill.: Quest Books, 1987.

Kriyananda, Swami. *Your Sun Sign as a Spiritual Guide*. Nevada City, Calif.: Ananda Publications, 1983.

Oken, Alan. *As Above, So Below*. New York: Bantam Books, 1973.

———. *The Horoscope, The Road and Its Travelers*. New York: Bantam Books, 1974.

Pagan, Isabelle M. *From Pioneer to Poet or the Twelve Great Gates: An Expansion of the Signs of the Zodiac Analyzed*. Wheaton, Ill.: The Theosophical Press, 1911.

Rudhyar, Dane. *Astrological Signs—The Pulse of Life*. Garden City, N.Y.: Doubleday and Co., Inc., 1963.

———. *The Astrological Houses*. Garden City, N.Y.: Doubleday and Co., Inc., 1972.

Sasportas, Howard. *The Twelve Houses*. London: The Aquarian Press, 1985.

CHAPTER 5

Arroyo, Stephen. *Astrology, Psychology, and the Four Elements: An Energy Approach to Astrology & Its Use in the Counseling Arts*. Sebastopol, Calif.: CRCS Publications, 1975.

Dione, Arthur. *Jungian Birth Charts: How to Interpret the Horoscope Using Jungian Psychology*. Wellingborough, England: The Aquarian Press, 1988.

Greene, Liz. *Relating: An Astrological Guide to Living with Others on a Small Planet*. York Beach, Maine: Samuel Weiser, Inc., 1978.

Greene, Liz, and Howard Sasportas. *Dynamics of the Unconscious: Seminars in Psychological Astrology, Volume 2*. York Beach, Maine: Samuel Weiser, Inc., 1988.

Guttman, Ariel, and Kenneth Johnson. *Mythic Astrology: Archetypal Powers in the Horoscope*. St. Paul, Minn.: Llewellyn Publications, 1993.

Jung, Carl G. "General Description of the Types." In *Psychological Types*. Volume 6 of the *Collected Works of C. G. Jung*. Princeton, N.J.: Princeton University Press, 1971.

————. "On Synchronicity." In *The Structure and Dynamics of the Psyche.* Volume 8 of the *Collected Works of C. G. Jung.* Princeton, N.J.: Princeton University Press, 1969.

Whitmont, Edward C. *The Symbolic Quest: Basic Concepts of Analytical Psychology.* Princeton, N.J.: Princeton University Press, 1978.

CHAPTER 6

Biedermann, Hans. *Dictionary of Symbolism: Cultural Icons and the Meanings Behind Them.* New York: NAL/Dutton, 1994.

George, Demetra. *Mysteries of the Dark Moon: The Healing Power of the Dark Goddess.* San Francisco: HarperCollins, 1992.

Greene, Liz, and Howard Sasportas. *The Luminaries: The Psychology of the Sun and Moon in the Horoscope: Seminars in Psychological Astrology, Volume 3.* York Beach, Maine: Samuel Weiser, Inc., 1992.

Guttman, Ariel, and Kenneth Johnson. *Mythic Astrology: Archetypal Powers in the Horoscope.* St. Paul, Minn.: Llewellyn Publications, 1993.

Rudhyar, Dane. *The Lunation Cycle.* Santa Fe, N.Mex.: Aurora Press, 1967.

Thompson, William Irwin. *The Time Falling Bodies Take to Light.* New York: St. Martin's Press, 1981.

CHAPTER 7

Graves, Robert. *The Greek Myths, Volumes 1 & 2.* London and New York: Penguin, 1960.

Greene, Liz, and Howard Sasportas. *The Development of the Personality: Seminars in Psychological Astrology, Volume 1.* York Beach, Maine: Samuel Weiser, Inc., 1987.

————. *The Inner Planets, Building Blocks of Personal Reality: Seminars in Psychological Astrology, Volume 4.* York Beach, Maine: Samuel Weiser, Inc., 1993.

Hine, D., trans. *The Homeric Hymns and the Battle of the Frogs and Mice.* New York: Atheneum, 1972.

Howell, Alice O. *Jungian Symbolism in Astrology.* Wheaton, Ill.: Quest Books, 1987.

Kerényi, Carl. *The Gods of the Greeks.* New York and London: Thames and Hudson Ltd., 1951.

Oken, Alan. *As Above, So Below*. New York: Bantam Books, 1973.

———. *The Horoscope, the Road and Its Travelers*. New York: Bantam Books, 1974.

CHAPTER 8

Abadie, M. J., and Claudia Bader. *Love Planets*. New York: Simon and Schuster, Inc., 1990.

Bolen, Jean Shinoda. *Goddesses in Everywoman: A New Psychology of Women*. New York: Harper and Row, 1984.

Dreyer, Ronnie Gale. *Venus: The Evolution of the Goddess and Her Planet*. San Francisco and London: HarperCollins, 1994.

Godolphin, Francis R. B., ed. *The Latin Poets*. New York: Random House, 1949.

Graves, Robert. *The Greek Myths, Volumes 1 & 2*. London and New York: Penguin, 1960.

Greene, Liz, and Howard Sasportas. *The Inner Planets, Building Blocks of Personal Reality: Seminars in Psychological Astrology, Volume 4*. York Beach, Maine: Samuel Weiser, Inc., 1993.

Howell, Alice O. *Jungian Symbolism in Astrology*. Wheaton, Ill.: Quest Books, 1987.

Otto, Walter F. *The Homeric Gods*. New York and London: Thames and Hudson Ltd., 1979.

CHAPTER 9

Bolen, Jean Shinoda. *Goddesses in Everywoman: A New Psychology of Women*. New York: Harper and Row, 1984.

———. *Gods in Everyman: A New Psychology of Men's Lives & Loves*. New York: Harper and Row, 1989.

Carriere, Jean-Claude, and Peter Brook, trans. *The Mahabharata*. New York: HarperCollins, 1987.

Cooper, J. C. *An Illustrated Encyclopaedia of Traditional Symbols*. New York and London: Thames and Hudson Ltd., 1978.

Greene, Liz. *Saturn: A New Look at an Old Devil*. York Beach, Maine: Samuel Weiser, Inc., 1976.

Howell, Alice O. *Jungian Symbolism in Astrology*. Wheaton, Ill.: Quest Books, 1987.

Kerényi, Carl. *The Gods of the Greeks*. New York and London: Thames and Hudson Ltd., 1951.

———. *Zeus and Hera: Archetypal Image of Father, Husband, and Wife*. Princeton, N.J.: Princeton University Press, 1975.

CHAPTER 10

Baigent, Michael, Nicholas Campion, and Charles Harvey. *Mundane Astrology: An Introduction to the Astrology of Nations and Groups*. Wellingborough, England: The Aquarian Press, 1984.

Chartrand, Mark R., III. *Skyguide: A Field Guide to the Heavens*. Racine, Wis.: Western Publishing Company, Inc., 1982.

Freud, Sigmund. "Repression." In *Collected Papers of Sigmund Freud, Volume IV*. New York: Basic Books, Inc., 1959.

———. "The Libido Theory." In *Collected Papers of Sigmund Freud, Volume V*. New York: Basic Books, Inc., 1959.

Greene, Liz. *The Astrological Neptune and the Quest for Redemption*. York Beach, Maine: Samuel Weiser, Inc., 1996.

———. *The Astrology of Fate*. York Beach, Maine: Samuel Weiser, Inc., 1984.

———. *The Outer Planets & Their Cycles: The Astrology of the Collective*. Sebastopol, Calif.: CRCS Publications, 1983.

Howell, Alice O. *Jungian Symbolism in Astrology*. Wheaton, Ill.: Quest Books, 1987.

Jung, Carl G. "The Aims of Psychotherapy." In *The Practice of Psychotherapy*. Volume 16 of the *Collected Works of C. G. Jung*. Princeton, N.J.: Princeton University Press, 1966.

Oken, Alan. *As Above, So Below*. New York: Bantam Books, 1973.

Sasportas, Howard. *The Gods of Change: Pain, Crisis and the Transits of Uranus, Neptune and Pluto*. London and New York: Penguin, 1989.

index